THE WRITER WITHIN

THE WRITER WITHIN

A Complete and Enjoyable Guide
to Writing from Everyday Life

Robert Wolf

Ruskin Press
Decorah, IA 52101

Copyright © 2013 by Robert Wolf. All rights reserved. Except for brief reviews, no part of this publication may be reproduced or transmitted in any form or by any means, electronic or mechanical, including Internet, photocopy, compact disc, recording, or any information or retrieval system without written permission from the publisher.
1. Writing Guide
ISBN: 0-9741826-2-1

Printed in the United States of America
on acid-free paper.

CONTENTS

	Introduction 1
CHAPTER ONE	Preliminary Matters 5
CHAPTER TWO	Strategies 17
CHAPTER THREE	Observation 31
CHAPTER FOUR	Genesis & Metamorphosis 55
CHAPTER FIVE	Conversation & Dialogue 73
CHAPTER SIX	Memoir Writing 99
CHAPTER SEVEN	Group Activities 117
	Bibliography 132

INTRODUCTION

The Writer Within is meant to be used by individuals and groups, in college classrooms, by the aspiring writer studying on his own, and by writing groups, whether teacherless or not. The exercises work best, however, when done with a group, for many rely on feedback and questions from others.

The Writer Within grew out of twenty years of teaching writing to people at all levels, from elementary school youngsters to college students to adults in community workshops. The foundation for the work grew by happenstance, when I began asking composition students at Roosevelt University in Chicago to tell the substance of their stories and essays to the class before writing them, to assure us that they had a strong theme with supporting details. One way for the class to discover potential strengths or weaknesses of the idea and/or story was to ask the teller questions about them. When neither were strong, the student would pick another theme or story. This laid the basis for what became an orally oriented method of writing instruction in which a telling, followed by class questions, always precedes writing.

This classroom experience in the late 1970s and early 1980s, was augmented simultaneously by my experience writing for Chicago theaters. The chapters on "Conversation and Dialogue" and "Group Activities" owe much to my collaborative experiences with actors and directors. And much of the spirit of play that I hope infuses the book comes from this experience. Both the classroom and theater experiences in turn contributed to the adult writing workshop that I began running for homeless men and women in Nashville, Tennessee in 1989. This, for me, was a turning point.

The workshop began accidentally, in a shelter for homeless

2 THE WRITER WITHIN

men, where I had been assigned by the Nashville Metro Board of Education to teach G.E.D. subjects to the shelter's residents. Since most of the men already had their G.E.D.s (some even had college degrees), I was told by my supervisor to improvise until the transient clientele changed. So I began talking with them in the common room, asking them how they became homeless, and soon I had them writing their stories. This was the commencement of the workshop, which soon expanded to include homeless women, and later aspiring writers from the Nashville community at large. It was an exciting group. After four months of writing we held a public reading, and a month after that the Board of Education published an anthology of workshop writings.

Eventually a friend and I decided to establish a non-profit press whose purpose would be to publish writings of the homeless. Free River Press was incorporated but it soon became clear that a publishing company that limited itself to homeless writings would not flourish. That, added to the fact that I had an insatiable desire to understand all aspects of American life, led me to expand Free River Press's mission to collect works from all regions of the country and by people from all walks of life. The goal then, was to develop and publish America's collective autobiography, written primarily by people without literary ambition.

Thus, when I moved to Iowa in 1991 I began working with farmers, and by the time the first farm book was published, it appeared in tandem with Free River Press's sixth volume by a homeless writer. Two more farm books followed, then volumes by small town residents. Along the way the press published a volume of fairy tales written by Iowa grade school youngsters, a memoir by a west Tennessee farmer, and a history of Chicago jazz. By that time Oxford University Press had expressed an interest in publishing an anthology of Free River Press writings, and in 1999 *An American Mosaic* appeared, with selections from writings by the homeless, by Midwest farmers and small town residents, and by people in the Mississippi Delta.

The majority of writing samples in this book come from people who participated in Free River Press writing workshops in various parts of the country. Only two samples did not—Rod Haynes's and Jack Hudson's pieces—and they were done long distance via mail and email. All the samples make clear that people without specialized training in composition, relying upon the innate wisdom of storytelling that we all have, and working in a group, can produce good and meaningful work.

The Writer Within is an introduction to a variety of forms. It begins with suggested exercises—the strategies in chapter two—to get the beginner writing. After that the exercises are focused primarily on observing the life around you: eavesdropping on conversations, listening for patterns of speech, taking notes on behavior and environment, and using these as the raw material for stories, one-act plays, essays, and novellas. Through these exercises in observation, the student is guided towards realism. This is obviously not the only route the beginner can take, but it is the easiest. The inspired student who is impelled to write eventually may explore fantasy and horror, surrealism and postmodernism. She may even explore an iconographic style that is the antithesis of detailed realism. But the method I am presenting will at least provide a solid foundation for other explorations.

The Writer Within is meant to be fun. Writing workshops and creative writing and composition classes that are non-competitive and mutually supportive are enriching environments: members learn techniques and grow in self-esteem. In such company, writing becomes play. It is what any artistic endeavor is ultimately about.

CHAPTER ONE
PRELIMINARY MATTERS

WRITING PRACTICE

Writing practice must be constant for growth to occur. Until you can set aside a regular period for it every day, your growth will be sporadic, at best.

Sometimes even people with a strong desire to write will go years before they make a routine or habit of writing for more than a half an hour a day. Know that if the desire to write is strong enough, and you are cursed or blessed with the need to write, you will eventually find yourself making time for it. It may take years for the need to manifest itself. The process of gestation is a mystery. The point to remember is that until you are writing regularly, your skills will not develop.

READING

Reading is just as important to the aspiring writer as consistent practice. Reading gives you an acquaintance with a variety of models in both style and form.

By studying style we gain, for example, an idea of possibilities for rhythm and sentence structure. We also learn something of the possibilities for expression: how thought is aided and limited by rhythmic and grammatical choices.

At whatever age you begin to think seriously of writing, that is the time to begin reading widely—novels, poems, plays, histories, biographies, essays, and short stories. At the moment you may be certain that you are destined to write novels, yet twenty years from now—if you're still writing—you may discover that your real form is the play or short poem or essay. Or you may find yourself writing in a variety of forms. But you can't discover which form or forms are yours until you've tried your hand at four or five— an essay, a short story, a free verse poem, perhaps a novella, a one-act play, a sonnet.

When you have developed familiarity with a variety of genres or forms of literature, you should begin to focus upon your favorite books, provided they are important. You should reread them until you know them intimately. I believe there is more to be gained by knowing a few important texts very well, than by having a superficial acquaintance with many.

Reflection

The writer needs to spend time thinking about language, forms, and genres. This means making your own examinations, rather than relying on the opinions of others. This is the analytical part of writing. It calls for a process of side-by-side comparison of literary models to understand their successes and failures.

One cannot create a novel or play intuitively. One must have read and thought about novels, and read, seen, and analyzed plays. A friend of mine had the habit of rereading a novel immediately after finishing it the first time. He read it first for enjoyment, and then again analytically, for fuller understanding.

However, some important elements of writing, such as sound and rhythm can only be acquired, I believe, by absorption. Sound and rhythm, because they are aural and therefore sensual, can only be fully apprehended or comprehended by the ear. The poet or composer can analyze a poem or musical composition into a series of stressed and unstressed accents or beats, and these can be broken into either feet and lines (poetry) or bars (music). But this analytic process is not the same as the creative process of laying down stresses and beats in the heat of composition or improvisation. The proof is in the fact that some of the greatest jazz musicians could not read music, and that great poetry has been composed in pre-literate cultures.

INSPIRATION AND REVISION

Jack Kerouac wanted his writing to reflect not only his past experience, but his consciousness during the act of writing. This meant (in theory) that he did not revise. The results, in some cases, are disastrous. Some writers are able to generate exciting work in a first draft, but this is a rarity. The art of writing can be said to reside in part in knowing when to conserve the beauty in the first draft, while revising that which needs reworking.

MEMORIZATION

Memorizing poems, dialogue, or narrative passages is out of vogue, yet memorizing portions of our favorite works and reciting them aloud to ourselves and others keeps rhythms and sounds in our heads. They begin to work unconsciously as we absorb them. We need to implant great lines in our memories that will serve as guides and echoes. I cannot overstress this point.

At a recent poetry reading by college students, some young writers, rather than read their own works, recited some of their favorite poems. And beautifully too. Their recitations reminded me of Dylan Thomas, who, when he gave public readings, included works by others.

THE SEARCH FOR RULES

I had one workshop participant decide that the way to learn to write short stories was to study formulas in how-to books. He was trying to create a well-crafted work, but he failed to write one decent story. He would have been better off reading several hundred short stories, thinking about them, and plunging in.

The same student was pleased to pass on to me the information that writers should never use more than twenty-five words in a sentence. He had picked up that advice from a how-to article. Here was a middle-aged man without a college education trying to learn to write. He was naturally susceptible to the claims of "experts."

This leads me to the following: beware of books that propose to give you rules. Beware of giving up your own quirkiness for someone else's strictures. Rely on your own first-hand inspections and your own creative drives.

Several decades ago an editor compiled a selection of readings by twentieth-century English speaking writers—including Hemingway, E.B. White, Jack Kerouac, Gertrude Stein, Thomas Wolfe, and others—followed by a critique of each writer's style. Now, if the editor's intention had been to demonstrate a variety of contemporary styles and to note important points of each, the book would have been worthwhile. But he happened to find one style—what we might call the E. B. White-*New Yorker* style— the standard against which all others must be judged. He heaped scorn upon Tom Wolfe, Pound, Kerouac, and others. He didn't like this writer's use of commas, or that one's use of a metaphor; he didn't like this person's rhythms or that one's choice of words. To this day I continue to read Pound, Hemingway, and Kerouac, but I cannot remember this man's name or the title of his book.

My point is this: the developed writer has his own voice, which means that his way of seeing the world and his expression are congruent: one reflects the other. His rhythms, syntax, punctuation and other elements will, to some degree, be idiosyncratic and reflect something of the writer's personality. When you read Pound's prose, you can hear Pound talking to you.

The Need for a Foundation

When I say, "Beware of rules," I say it with this provision: you must learn standard grammatical practice before you begin experimenting. Do not think that ignorance of standard usage is acceptable in business writing or that it will get you published. It will not. There is a variety of styles of punctuation and sometimes syntax among established writers, but they have achieved their styles by hard practice. Bad grammar is not the same as literary experimentation, and an article or poem that is written in ignorance of standard usage is unlikely to get published. Before you begin experiments with word order or quirky punctuation, learn to write standard English.

Let me make the point another way. One of the best tips on writing I ever received came from the eminent anatomy instructor,

Robert Beverly Hale, who lectured on anatomy at the Art Students League and at Columbia University, where I took his course. He told us, "Before you start distorting the figure, learn to draw it accurately. Learn to draw like the Renaissance and Baroque masters." Or words to that effect.

Learn to write simple expository prose. Study grammar and usage from a standard text. If you have already done this on your own or in school, you are ready to develop your own voice.

LEARNING THROUGH IMITATION

Before you find your own voice, which means developing a style that reflects your sensibility, you will almost inevitably find yourself imitating your favorite writer. This is typical: the creative person, whether a musician, painter, writer, or sculptor, almost always learns his craft by imitating a favorite in his field.

Learning through imitation is best illustrated by the medieval guild system, in which the neophyte, the apprentice, was bound by contract to a master for so many years. The Renaissance workshops, north and south, grew out of the guild system. Not only the great Italian painters of the Renaissance, but northern artists like Albrecht Durer, learned their art at the hands of a teacher. The early work of both Leonardo and Durer shows the influence of their respective masters.

Rather than list painters, composers, and writers, and their influences, I will give this one anecdote. The great tenor saxist Bud Freeman and his young jazz musician friends in the Austin High Gang spent several years in the 1920s studying the music of Louis Armstrong and Bix Beiderbecke. Several times a week they would travel from their suburban homes to Chicago's South Side to listen to the two masters play in night clubs and dance halls. Some of the gang preferred Armstrong, others Beiderbecke. Freeman would tell his friend, cornetist Jimmy McPartland, "You've got too much Beiderbecke in your playing," and McPartland would retort, "You've got too much Armstrong." Freeman went on to develop his own idiosyncratic style with intricate, loopy phrasing, which in turn became the inspiration for Lester Young's style.

Postscript

As you begin writing keep in mind that with constant practice you will improve, provided that you read good models, think about them, memorize favorite parts, and even imitate the style of some of your models. You need the occasional company of other writers, too, but be leery of their critiques. Even accurate observations can have a negative effect if not stated diplomatically. You must maintain a delicate balancing act between trusting your own intuitions and listening to what others have to say about your work. In the end, a writer must have thick skin, accept some criticism, and plunge on. The exercises in the next chapter will get the process going.

CHAPTER TWO
STRATEGIES

This chapter discusses a few methods you can use to get started writing, or to free yourself from writer's block, or to explore new possibilities. Some demand a lot of time, but then the serious aspirant devotes a lot of time to learning the craft.

STORY TELLING

Story telling is one way of sorting out the elements of a story we want to write. When I run workshops, I have participants tell their stories and then answer questions about them. Finally, I tell them to write their stories as closely as they can to the way they told them. This advice, to copy oral tellings, takes the mystery out of writing.

As a youngster growing up in Connecticut I used to listen one night a week to Jean Shepherd tell stories on WOR radio in New York. The friend who turned me on to him thought this was great stuff. But to my mind Shepherd rambled on too much, talking primarily about his boyhood in Gary, Indiana with lots of unrelated musings thrown in. While I don't remember particular stories, I do recall that he spoke very dramatically, sometimes with great emphasis, as though speaking in italics or in capital letters. He would bring his voice down to a whisper and speak with great intensity when he wanted to underline a point. Or he might, all of a sudden, boom the punch line. His voice was the best part of the evening. Many times he would leave story telling altogether and ramble on about an idea. Once he asked his listeners to imagine that their lives were pies and to consider how big a slice would be cut for goofing off, how much for work, etc.

What Shepherd was doing, although unintentionally I'm sure, was preparing to write his stories. He was sorting events out, discovering what was dramatic, what worked, what didn't. (Plenty of other writers, including Sherwood Anderson and Jack Kerouac, have used story telling as a way of preparing themselves to write.) Fifteen or so years later Shepherd's stories began appearing in magazines, and have been extremely effective models to use in workshops. They are filled with exaggeration, with long pauses indicated by dots (..........!!!!!), with capitalized or italicized words to make a point. They are very visual. They encourage writers to exaggerate and to have fun with typography, using it to make their point by indicating how the words should be read.

Years ago I learned that the more prewriting exercises that students have, the more fluently they will write. Thus when I run workshops, we spend more time on prewriting exercises than on the writing itself, and story telling is one exercise I use consistently, for it not only helps students to identify the stories they want to write, but to explore them too. But before they write, I have other workshop members ask them about their stories. I will suggest, "Is there anything you want to know more about?" This can cover anything from what was said in a conversation to a description of the physical surroundings to details of any action involved. These questions help the author to relive the story, and in reliving it, to tell it more fully.

Exercise
If you are in a class or a teacherless writing group, take turns telling stories and helping the tellers know what you want to know more about. Perhaps you will want to know what was actually said by people in the story, not just the topic of the conversation. Or perhaps you will want to know how the teller felt in this or that situation. If you are not part of a class or group, pick a story from your life and tell it to someone. Ask them what else they want to know: anything about the action, conversation, characters and place. After this sorting out, write it down.

SPONTANEOUS PROSE COMPOSITION

"Spontaneous prose composition" is the name Jack Kerouac gave to a free-wheeling yet sometimes controlled process by which he generated most of his works, and which he explained in a brief essay, "Essentials of Spontaneous Prose Composition." In it, Kerouac exhorted the reader to write from "the jewel-center of mind," meditating upon an event or thing in a semi-trance. The aim of the method is to work in a steady rush, not stopping to search for the right word or to think about grammar. The writer is to compose in "breaths," like a jazz musician, and when he comes to the end of a breath (or thought) to close it with a dash. Kerouac advised the writer to avoid using commas and semi-colons, advice he himself seldom followed.

At its best, as in his novella *The Subterraneans,* in portions of *Visions of Cody* or in "Railroad Earth," his object, be it an event or person, sometimes disappears as Kerouac is reminded of something tangential to it and explains the tangential matter in a parenthetical aside. As one critic said, the heart of the writing seems to lie in these asides, which are showing us the flow of Kerouac's mind as he works. The method did not always succeed, and to my mind it failed more often than not. It presumes that honesty (first association) will always produce interesting work, which it does not. Confession can become babbling.

Here is a brief excerpt that gives a hint of Kerouac at his best. The second paragraph of *The Subterraneans* begins:

> I was coming down the street with Larry O'Hara old drinking buddy of mine from all the times in San Francisco in my long and nervous and mad careers I've gotten drunk and in fact cadged drinks off friends with such "genial" regularity nobody really cared to notice or announce that I am developing or was developing in my youth, such bad freeloading habits though of course they did notice but liked me and as Sam said "Everybody comes to you for your gasoline boy, that's some filling station you got there" or say words to that effect—

Kerouac feels free to talk about his drinking, his freeloading, and what others say about him. All of which I think would be less interesting if written in conventional prose in as short a space. Kerouac makes it work because he has found his voice.

This is the kind of freedom you should experience when writing a first draft. Everything should be a candidate for the hopper. If you decide to edit later, then edit. In workshops I do not encourage students to go into a semi-trance or to write from "the jewel center of mind," for I want them to concentrate more on the event and not to exhibit or explore tangential matters.

I have used Kerouac's method in my own writing and it has produced some brief but good passages. My problem has been knowing when not to rewrite, for like many other writers I have a fear of following my impulses when they run counter to accepted practice.

Exercise
Scan your mind for an event that you have been bursting to tell—a story that arouses strong emotions. Now visualize it. Then pick some point in the action and start writing. As you write, continue to see the activity you describe. If an idea or thought about one of the characters or about an object in the area grabs your attention, write about it until drawn back to the main event. Whenever your mind is drawn away from the story let it follow the flow of association.
Do not worry about spelling or punctuation. Do not stop to consider whether you have chosen the right word, just write. Do not stop writing until you are either tired or have come to the end of the subject. In fact, do not try to force your words into conventional form; forget about rules. Forget about periods and commas if you wish. If you chose, leave out all punctuation.

FREE WRITING

Related to Kerouac's spontaneous prose composition is what Peter Elbow has called "free writing," a process he outlined in his book, *Writing without Teachers*. Free writing does not attempt to focus on any object at all, as does spontaneous prose composition, but simply follows the mind's associations, writing them down, omitting nothing. It came at a time when English instructors in schools and colleges were covering student compositions with red marks that corrected grammatical and spelling errors. This implanted a nasty editor inside the head of anyone who had suffered under this instruction, making them fearful of setting words to paper. I remember many times—even years after I had left school—simply sitting frozen because I was not sure whether or not a comma belonged in a certain place, whether I had chosen the right word, and so on. Elbow's book was partially responsible for the fact that teachers now routinely have students write their first drafts in one uninterrupted rush. Kerouac probably influenced the change too.

In his brief chapter on free writing, Elbow discussed how the writer can use three or four free writing exercises to construct an essay, but, by the nature of free writing, it is a lengthy process. Briefly, free writing is ideal for anyone who wants to write but can't, and isn't sure how to get unstuck. Here's an example:

Vacuum cleaner in the background, humidifier humming, computer keys clicking you write about whatever is in your surroundings just keep writing for as long as you can until something clicks in do you understand??? Yes, that is very clear now back to what's here in the environment in the room, the computer screen my hands hitting keys on the keyboard there's the vacuum cleaner again I don't like that irritating sound but what can you do? I'll tell you what think about the day outside the gray sky the damp air the wind blowing slowly through the trees the grass is greening the boughs of pines look droopy and I'm here inside trying to write and write and I'm running out of ideas what about you? what about it? What are you going to do?

Exercise
If you are having trouble finding an object to write about, or are fearful of focusing, practice free writing ten minutes a day for a week. Simply write down the free associations that pop into your mind. The mind, eventually tired of babbling, will focus on an object and kick in.

16 THE WRITER WITHIN

You can use free writing to explore a broad, predetermined subject area. Let us suppose you are searching for a specific subject within the range of items, but have not narrowed anything down, have not found anything that inspires you. Simply free write: put down an association of ideas until the mind clicks on a topic. Here is a sample of free writing done by Jerry Crabb in a workshop in Helena, Arkansas. The assignment was to write something about the Mississippi Delta.

> Stream-of-consciousness—town—pain—untapped memories—characters—where does interest lie?—whose interest? whose ox is being gored? oxen on Cherry Street? photo—Gladin's studio—AA meetings—generations collide—Star Trek, the Next Generation—"Beam, Me Up, Scottie!—"I tell you, captain, she can't handle it!" TV's impact—what of the South via mass communication? Where were the Beverly Hillbillies from? Tennessee? Tennessee Ford? Tennessee Williams? What did Tennessee? Why is Tennessee a Southern state? Is Al Gore Southern? What is a Southerner? Is the tenant farmer of Depression days more Southern than this vice-president son of a U.S. senator? Who makes the rules? Is Dick Smith less Southern for his pre-1977 roots?
>
> What, I ask myself, is the most Southern of movies? Is it *Gone with the Wind*? or something else? And why is the Civil War always at the bottom of our search for the Southern character? What would Shelby Foote say?
>
> And is eastern Arkansas more or less Southern than western Arkansas? Did cotton somehow fashion a more truly Southern culture? Why is Phillips County today a predominantly black county?

The writer was slowly moving about the idea of the Southern character: what it was and what made it. With his final question about Phillips County, his mind lit on the image of black people, and of his nanny. On another page he made a few fast notes. "Surrogate mother—effort to sit and eat at the table—not allowed to sit at the table—movies suggested colored vs. whites only." Then he began:

> Lovey Johnson was our black mama. She helped raise the four of us with the threatened discipline of a green switch coupled with innumerable helpings of corn bread and navy beans. She was one of an endless stream of surrogate mothers in the segregated South. . . .
> The black nanny had by the 1950's long been a Southern institution. Even the poorest, most down-on-their-luck white family such as ours could often afford a black maid-cum-babysitter such as Lovey so very low were the wages that a black worker of that day might expect. How Lovey ever managed to survive is one of my life's mysteries.

Exercise
If you have a subject for a story or essay but don't know how to tackle it, free write until the mind focuses. Once the story or train of ideas starts, don't worry about plot or sequential development of ideas, simply follow the convolutions of your mind, as in spontaneous prose composition.

READING ALOUD

Reading your work and the work of good authors aloud is important to your growth as a writer. First, it helps develop the rhythmic sense, for only a good ear can develop good rhythms. There is probably a limitation to what anyone can do: we are born with certain equipment and probably cannot exceed our inheritance. But not to read aloud is to not develop whatever innate gift we have.

We need good models: good voices that can modulate in pitch and volume, that know when to linger over a word or when to pick up the pace. Many writers are lackluster readers who speak in a monotone, have no sense of drama, and no connection with the audience.

So how does one begin to experience the drama of the page? First, by hearing great actors or great poets read. I was fortunate, when growing up, to live in the vicinity of New York City and would go on weekends to see plays. I was particularly intrigued by the Phoenix APA, an off-Broadway theater that consistently ran strong productions. It was there I first saw the American actor Donald Madden, who performed the best Hamlet I have ever seen. His raptures, as the poet Drayton said of Marlowe's lines, "were all air and fire." It is performances like his that stay with you, usually dormant but ready to come alive to remind us of the beauty and power that language can achieve.

If you cannot see great theater live, then get recordings of Shakespeare's plays on CD or DVD. Watch and listen to the great British actors. Make every effort to find copies of recordings made by Carl Sandburg and Dylan Thomas of their own poetry. These men had a sense of the dramatic. Follow their words on the printed page as you listen to them. Read the poems aloud yourself, and see how you would inflect the words.

One of the best gifts I ever received was a recording of Thomas reading his work. I played the recording over and over until I absorbed his rhythms and sense of language. I would declaim my own nonsense poetry in the Thomas style created extempore, shouted out when no one could hear. I had to allow myself the freedom to stumble and stay stupid things but I had to go on. Soon I got over any hesitancy and let the rhythms dictate whatever nonsense popped into my head. I repeated the same exercise with Sandburg until I could improvise sequences of Sandburg sounding lines.

As you are listening and imitating great readings or performances, begin reading your own works aloud. Seeing the images in the poem or story, communicate them in your reading. Communicate the verbs. If the work describes a fast activity, speed up the voice. But listen to recordings of yourself. You may think that you are reading intelligibly when you are galloping along. This is a common problem.

Another thing you can do as you read your own works, is to try to listen objectively. Try to hear another's voice reading to you. This may help you identify awkward spots. Better than that is to have a friend who reads well, read it to you.

Note that when beginning writers read their work to others they sometimes insert words, even sentences, that they omitted on the page. I have seen this many times in workshops, and I have seen the same writers later fail to insert the interpolations when they revised their work. This, I think, is because when we read the works ourselves we are not fully aware of the gaps, which stand out unmistakably when another reads it to us. Further, hearing another read our work we become more readily aware of any awkwardness. When a friend reads your work, have her read exactly what you have written. She's not doing you a favor by filling in missing words or correcting tense or number.

Exercises
1. *Either through stores, or the Internet, or inter-library loans, get audio or visual dramatizations of several Shakespeare productions. Read Shakespeare's text first, then listen to the actors' interpretations. Practice reading some of the great speeches from these plays: Richard III's opening monologue, Henry V's famous address to the troops at Agincourt, and Lear's first soliloquy upon the heath and that in Act V as he carries the dead Cordelia in his arms.*
2. *If you can, compare performances of the same play. There are several versions of Hamlet and Richard III available on DVD.*
3. *Caedmon records issued numerous recordings of prominent poets reading their own work. Get hold of those if you can, particularly those by Sandburg and Thomas, both very dramatic readers. Select certain poems from the recordings and read them aloud to yourself.*
4. *Make a habit of reading aloud for at least fifteen minutes a day. Whenever you read poetry—lyric, narrative or dramatic —read it aloud. In a play, take all the parts.*
5. *Read several of your stories or poems to a friend.*
6. *Have that friend read your work to you.*

SKETCHING

One of Kerouac's friends, Ed White, suggested that Kerouac practice the verbal equivalent of artistic sketching. As an architecture student White had carried small sketch pads to help him remem-

20 THE WRITER WITHIN

ber what he saw. Kerouac took the advice and carried pocket-sized notebooks to record whatever caught his attention. Among the published examples were descriptions of a New York cafeteria, an ancient men's room at a Third Avenue El stop, the exterior of a B-run movie house on 42nd Street, and the front window of a pastry shop. But instead of limiting himself to description, Kerouac allows himself to free associate. Thus, in the course of describing a cafeteria in *Visions of Cody*, he mentions a man reading a newspaper, who reminds him of an Arab, and furthermore, because of the hair sticking out from under his hat reminds him of Aly Khan. "He sits semi-facing cafeteria (where us Egyptians wait) under this damn 20-foot door that looks like it's going to open behind him and a green monstrous 5-foot-hand will come out, wrap around his chair and slide him in . . ."

Sketches can obviously be left in first draft form as records of observations, or polished and reworked.

Like the other exercises in this section, sketching can help you get over dry spells when you can't think of anything to write. With sketching, one's immediate environment becomes a great opportunity for making records. Many times the great painters chose the life around them for their subjects. Think of the humble objects that Van Gogh painted: his yellow room at Arles, his shoes, Gauguin's armchair, potatoes, and so on. Writers too. Think of Sherwood Anderson, who grew up in a small Ohio town, later writing stories inspired by it. Let the writer who is beginning on his journey practice with the life around him.

Here is a sketch written by computer programmer Ron Kittleman for a writing workshop in La Crosse, Wisconsin, after the group had read some of Kerouac's sketches. This was written outside the downtown post office.

He limps slightly in T-shirt white with checked shorts reaches for the door and out strides a petite woman in yellow blouse staring straight ahead so no one notices her or she notices no one the long pony tailed dark haired man strutting in goatee and motorcycle jacket denim with patches all walk spritely in the brown brick square stark walkway the pink shirt lady hurrying letters in hand the old man waddles short eternal steps as cars pass approach the stop sign stands with a tilt to the right no one notices some don't ever stop the mural like terra cotta image some baroque scene of cherubs and angels and naked children climbing trees orange and white barricades with yellow tape warning the little old lady with stick green rain jacket plaid skirt black walking shoes and a velvet fuzzy coat— she turned to look as I saw her hat or maybe the sound of the bouncing trailer behind the pickup ignoring the stop sign.

Exercises
Each day for two weeks find a different place to sketch. For example, sit at a lunch counter and observe what is happening. Write your observations as fast as you can. Note conversations, but do not try to notate them word for word. Get a few broad strokes, note the gist of the conversation, a few exchanges; mainly concentrate on the ambiance—the look and feel of the place. Is the physical setting mirrored in the look and gestures of the customers? What details of the physical setting are you drawn to? Is it very modern with clean lines or old and rundown? Note what the servers look like. Do they reflect the place? If there is a short order cook, what are his gestures? Is he clean? Is his apron greasy? What does he look like? How does he stand, straight or slouched? Does he talk much? Loudly? Any peculiar accent?

Keep the sketches varied: a street scene, a coffee shop, a bar, a gym, a nightclub, an office, etc. In some, focus on process and activity; in others focus on place. If you live in the city, you can describe your neighborhood in a succession of fourteen sketches, each from a different perspective. If you live in the country, you have the opportunity to sketch animals and the natural environment.

SKETCHING AS NOTETAKING

Describing activity in a café is one thing, describing an action event is another. The slow paced activity of a cafe (unless you're recording conversation) can allow you to write sentences, but a professional wrestling match, for example, is too fast for that and what you will get are a series of notes you need to flesh out later. For years I was a professional wrestling fan, and in fact the first story I ever sold to the *Chicago Tribune* was a large piece on wrestling. The following selection from the notes was later transformed into the story's first six paragraphs.

> M. Hayes AWA champ   red sequined floor length robe, blue stripes crisscrossing w/ stars   blond hair, brown beard "Am I beautiful or what?" Rick Martel comes up   hero enters crowd goes wild— the champ is confused— Why aren't they clapping for me? Hero w/ belt on mat, throws off belt & goes at Hayes Hayes poses on ropes, head high, hands on hips. They LOVE Martel, LIKED Hayes. Hayes one leg forward struts around stage hands out palms up crowd loves Hayes struts walks back so smoothly poses muscles hand up preens woman: Asshole! (w/ newspaper up held.)

The *Tribune* piece began:

> "Bad Street USA" is blaring over the speakers and the Rosemont Horizon crowd is on its feet, straining for a look at the man in the floor-length red, white and blue sequined cape walking up one of the aisles. His female admirers are clapping and screaming as he climbs into the ring, jerks his head up, brushes back his locks and begins strutting in slow steps around the mat.
>
> Yes, this is Michael Hayes from Bad Street, U.S.A., and now he's raising his arms above his head and shouting, "Am I beautiful or what?"
>
> The music on the speakers changes. Hayes is standing on the ropes in the glare of spotlights, looking into the crowd, head held high, his long golden hair curling over his shoulders. The crowd is still applauding him, but its enthusiasm is dimmed. Its attention now is focusing on Rick Martel, the American Wrestling Association [AWA] heavyweight champ making his way quickly up the aisle.
>
> Hayes seems confused, jerking his head around, walking back and forth across the ring, frowning and wondering

what's happening. Poor Hayes doesn't understand the reason until Martel gets in the ring.
Something is wrong. Martel pays no attention to his screaming fans or to the preening Hayes, who is trying to regain the crowd's attention. No, Martel takes off his championship belt, throws it on the mat and attacks Hayes FROM BEHIND! Martel is clearly upset! For a good guy like Martel to attack Hayes from behind without warning, without waiting for the referee to begin the match, means that Hayes must have done something really bad.
The crowd is roaring. This is the last match of the evening and the excitement has built steadily for the last 2 1/2 hours to this frenzied pitch. The fans have seen one of their heroes left unconscious on the mat. They have seen the rules broken by good guys and bad guys, heads smashed into turnbuckles, and now—horror of horrors!—baby face Martel's sudden attack is being repulsed by Hayes.
Hayes is body slamming Martel again and again onto the mat. Martel just lies there and Hayes jumps onto the top ropes in a corner and poses, his head held high, his hands on his hips. Then he begins strutting around the stage in those small, prancing steps of his, hands out, palms up, as if to say, "Look at how beautiful I am." A small, good-looking woman in a second-row seat is standing up, her face a mask of hatred, waving a rolled-up newspaper and shouting obscenities at Hayes.

There is much in the story that is not in the notes, but I wrote the story the day after the match while the sights and sounds and sequence of events were still clear in my mind. You will hear writer after writer advise about the need to type up notes as soon as possible after taking them.

Exercise
Pick a fast moving activity—crowds moving through a department store, work at a construction site, a sporting event—and take notes. If you have access to a factory, describe the work. No later than the next

day write up your notes.

SKETCHIING FROM MEMORY

A useful drawing exercise is to recollect an event or image that made a great impression on you and to draw it from memory.

The following is an excerpt from an unrevised sketch written in the Nashville homeless writing workshop by Ed Ritter after participants and I had read aloud passages from *Visions of Cody*. In this and another sketch, the writer decided not only to omit commas but periods too.

> The time is 4:30 sharp you're standing in line waiting to get a meal ticket if you want to call it a meal— The men in this line looking like cows being herded into a cattle truck some look as if they haven't had a bath in weeks there's a lot of chatter name-calling pushing shoving sometimes actual fights all this so you stand in yet another line to eat food that no sane person would touch yet it beats starving barely that is you're there crowded into a room filled with tables that look like they should be thrown out you sit like a bunch of vultures going over food that looks like something that even they wouldn't eat so bad at times that you can hear people asking each other what it is but nobody can give a definite answer to the question the men in this place are diverse there's frank the philosopher he says well a pretty good meal today yeah if slop is your idea of good others look at the food and say damn there must be a better way to eat than this while yet others just sit quietly and eat because griping does no good the food is so bad you see many guys throw half of it away then go outside to have their after dinner smoke tailor made if they have them if not roll your own sometimes four or five guys share one pack of tobacco if you haven't guessed this is not a restaurant or a normal person's home the meal I'm describing is being served at the Mission

The writer wrote a very accurate account while not moving into particulars, except to mention "frank the philosopher." Still,

I can envision the line of men, the food, and hear the comments. A different kind of memory sketch can be done by focusing on particulars. Here is one that a friend, Arthur Welsh, wrote immediately after leaving mass.

July 16
Church of Christ the Redeemer— designed by Palladio— paintings by Tintoretto, Bassano, Bistiano— Mass 10:00 a.m. Saturday— ten minutes after service begins and the chanting is filling the vault a well dressed woman, green blouse & white shirt comes in with a boy— The boy is bullish, four feet ten, let's say, stocky— thick neck & barrel chest, hair cropped to ears curling like Renaissance style wearing red & blue stripped T-shirt and blue jeans shorts— He & woman (mother?) come up the center aisle— The boy continues to lurch forward after the mother has stopped, makes sounds, "Awk! awk!" — The woman grabs him and leads him to a bench—He sits quietly for awhile— then gawks, snapping his deformed face to look behind him— thick, protrudent lips, heavy cheeks, eyes gazing without focus— bull neck with muscles flowing into thick shoulders— Snaps head around— I avert my gaze so as not to get him excited and afraid and awking in fear— At one point he stood up at an inappropriate time of the service, his mother pulled him down— at another, when all were standing he's hitting an imaginary antagonist at his side, chopping him with the flat of his hand, the fuck you to the same— Later crosses himself for no reason— fouls it up— misses one of the points of the cross— also has no order to it, does it diagonally.
    Furthermore his gawking is like paranoia— looking to see who's staring at him— not to inspect people or architecture— Spent considerable time at one point (while we're all standing) tucking his shirt in— which he does compulsively with fast jabs at the shirt— and then spends much time hiking his pants up. Charles Laughton as the Hunchback of Notre Dame, only no hump—

Exercise
Observe an event carefully without taking notes or sketching. Five to ten minutes later write it up.

EAVESDROPPING

When we practice eavesdropping we begin to pay attention to different speech patterns, hopefully to the point where we can phonetically reproduce whatever we hear. This has several uses besides the ability to write convincing dialogue. First, it is a simple way to begin writing, for unless the conversation is very slow or you know shorthand, you are bound to have gaps in your notes. Filling these in, based on memory, is an excellent focusing exercise for writing dialogue. Second, the recorded conversation can be used to construct a story based on one or more participants in the conversation. This, obviously, is because an interesting conversation will be a key to character. Use eavesdropping as an opportunity to study character.

Listen for pauses, emphases, and repeated words or phrases. Watch the gestures that accompany words, and the physical attitude of the speakers. How do all these elements work into a whole?

Exercise
Go to a public place with a small notebook. To disguise your intentions, bring a book with you. Open it and pretend to be taking notes from the book as you eavesdrop. Go to five very different places and transcribe as much of the conversation as you can. Go back to your computer as soon as you can and transcribe the notes, filling in whatever words you missed, based on memory or likely guesswork.

REWRITING PUBLIC DOMAIN MATERIAL

It is not uncommon for writers to rewrite public domain material, though it is less common today than in the past. Consider playwrights: most great playwrights do not invent their own plots. The Greek tragedians took their stories from mythology; Plautus and Terence rewrote the plays of Menander; the Elizabethans, including Shakespeare, got their stories from histories, novellas, and preexisting plays; and Brecht used history and other plays for the basis of many of his works.

The 1996 best-seller by Jane Smiley, *A Thousand Acres*, about an Iowa farmer and his daughters, was a retelling of *King Lear*. Tennessee Williams and Jean Cocteau both rewrote the Orpheus myth; Thomas Wolfe used the myth of Antaeus for a large section of *Of Time and the River*; Joyce retold the story of Odysseus' wanderings; and more recently, forty-two poets have reinterpreted passages from Ovid's *Metamorphoses* in the anthology *After Ovid*, some staying close to the text, others using Ovid as a springboard for wild departures. Of course, rewriting public domain material is not limited to the classics, but they seem to offer the most conspicuous examples.

In our time the English poet Christopher Logue is slowly writing an adaptation of the *Iliad*, which may some day be acknowledged one of the great poetic achievements of the twentieth and twenty-first centuries. Critics and others who call his work a translation are mistaken. Logue has taken the bare bones of the *Iliad*'s story, everything else is his own. Some portions of Homer's narrative he cuts, others he greatly expands, sometimes with dialogue or detailed cinematic description. (The latest installment of his work creates entire scenes that Homer doesn't hint at.) And all this is done in brief sentences sometimes amounting to single words, brutal imagery, fast cuts, and contemporary speech. Here is a real poet working.

Exercises
1. *Take a tale from the collection of the brothers Grimm and translate it into a contemporary story.*
2. *Find an old ballad that you like and transform it into a short story or a tale told in free verse.*
3. *Take a story from the Bible and rework it into a contemporary tale.*

RECORDING DREAMS
Most of us do not remember dreams on a regular basis. To do

so we must write them down. Keep a notebook by the bedside, and if you are awakened by a dream, write it down. Write down what you remember on awakening. At first you may not remember much, but once you begin writing down the occasional dreams you do recall, you will begin remembering more.

Keeping a dream journal has other advantages besides offering an incentive to write. Aside from whatever insight, if any, they may give you to your inner life, dream journaling is important for three reasons. First, it is another form of writing, and during the early stages of your writing the more you do, of any kind, the better. Second, dreams offer several literary devices to use in your work. They are filled with exaggeration, with impossibilities, with cinematic cuts. Third, dreams themselves are keys to the unconscious and, I think, are underused by fiction writers. They add another dimension to your characters.

Here's one from workshop participant George Ellis.

> I step out of a freight elevator along with other people & the doors start to shut & I see a baby in a stroller there & struggle to stop the massive doors. I do keep them open.
> My girlfriend (some nameless nitwit) says, "Oh, leave it alone."
> I say, "No, we have to find its mother."
> "Oh," she says, "it'll be alright. Someone will find it."
> For a moment I think the baby may be okay, the elevator can go up another floor where its mother will be waiting for it. Think no. Walk off to get help. Girlfriend stays.
> I'm in a department store which becomes a bar or social club, thinking to get hold of my friends who can help. A male friend is with me. I say, "I'm calling Hemingway." This is his hangout & we're his pals, but hearing myself say it I sound like a showoff. (My friend and I are young but famous.) I want to go to the phone booth and call Hemingway who's in Key West but realize he probably won't come cause we're in Miami and that's too long a trip for the boat.

Here's the opening of a dream from Fred, who taught school:

Lost all my friends. First I'd been hanging out in the cafeteria and teachers' lounge of a grade school where my friends are talking. Then one of them comes over and tells me I'm not welcome any more because I'm too loud.
"Every time you come here you make a lot of noise, Fred."
I'm shamed. I didn't know that. All I know is that I like to laugh. Maybe my laugh was too loud.
"Too many imitations."
Oh, yes. I remember I imitate different voices, different people. They didn't like that.
Then I'm riding in a taxi with Bill Sharp. We stop, get out, I give Bill a dollar to pay for my share. As the taxi pulls away Bill angrily tells me I didn't pay my share, that I never do. He doesn't want me over at his house, caging meals from him and Jean. I slink away.
Next my father and mother are giving it to me for some reason . . .

Exercise
Keep a dream journal for at least three weeks. At first you may not remember any, then fragments, then, as you practice recalling and writing them down, you will find yourself remembering more and more dreams.

IMITATION

Learning by imitation is a fairly universal process for musicians, composers, artists and writers. By imitating your favorite writers you understand how they achieved their effects. By reading a few of their works repeatedly you begin to understand how they used language—their characteristic rhythms, metaphors, dialogue, and so on. Understanding four or five diverse writers well will provide an important education.

Exercises
1. Write a story or essay in imitation of one of your favorite

authors. Pick a theme and/or characters that typify this writer.

2. Take a published story with well-defined characters and a strong narrative and rewrite it in imitation of one of your favorite authors. As you do this you will find yourself changing the characters and story line.

CHAPTER THREE
OBSERVATION

Practiced writers who succeed in creating realistic scenes and characters have a store of impressions they can use when needed. Sometimes, of course, it is harder to reach into the memory and pull out what you want, but with practice the job becomes easier. The realist must, first of all, watch and listen to the world carefully enough to collect a very large store of impressions—images of people, activities, and places, as well as records of conversations.

OBSERVING WITHOUT THOUGHT

Learn to observe without judging, without letting thought intrude between you and the object. One way to practice wordless observation is to watch a thing or activity with the intent of remembering it in detail a year from now. You won't, of course, but that is the kind of intensity that is needed. I believe it was Picasso who advised painters "to make yourself think in photographs." Wordless observation is different from the observation in which we measure and judge experiences against one another. The fact that we are not normally close observers is shown in conflicting eyewitness accounts of the same event.

THE NEED FOR EXPERIENCE

A comment on the American painter Thomas Hart Benton will hopefully drive home the point about the importance of observation and experience. In the 1930s Benton painted four major murals, the first of which was a panorama of American life based on sketches he had made on trips through the South, the West, and the Middle West, as well as those made during sojourns in Chicago and New York. Benton had gotten to know these places well. He had tramped and driven through Appalachia and Ozark country, known the folk, attended their tent revivals and drunk their moonshine. He had sketched workers in Gary, Indiana steel mills and West Virginia mines; he had drawn cotton pickers bending with their sacks in Delta fields, and roustabouts loading bales of cotton on Mississippi steamboats. He visited oil boom towns in Texas and Oklahoma, bunked with cowboys in New Mexico, sketched rodeo riders in Wyoming. In the Middle West, his home region, he had drawn life on the farm and in small towns. He had studied life, high and low, in the big city.

All these observations came together in his mural, *America Today*, created for the New School for Social Research in 1930-31. Working directly from his sketches, the figures and activities in the mural reflect what Benton saw, down to the details of the individual expressions of his subjects. The mural has extraordinary power and vitality. The angular figures, caught in work or recreation, are always in motion and cram the six panels. Groups of figures are marked off from one another by flat planes, or by the molding of the frame extending into the composition.

By 1936, when Benton came to paint his third mural, *A Social History of Missouri*, he no longer relied on sketches and first-hand observations. His figures are less individuated. The mural covers far more space than *America Today*, and instead of abruptly juxtaposing groups of figures, he relates them through perspective. The largest panel, covering 20 x 60 feet, is a tour de force, with five vanishing points. Formally it is astounding. It has been called his best mural, but I do not think so. It lacks life.

Instead of basing it on drawings and observations, Benton worked from molded figures he created for the composition. This became his method in subsequent years. By the time he painted his murals in the 1950s and 60s, he was no longer trying to reflect life. His two large panels executed for the Power Authority of the State of New York, and his mural for the Truman Library in Independence, Missouri are both historical. The figures are arranged in tableaus; both are set pieces, and to my mind they are lifeless and unconvincing.

In his autobiography Benton admitted that he eventually gave up painting contemporary scenes because he became incapable of understanding the social meanings of what he saw. Consequently he no longer felt comfortable insinuating himself into conversations among strangers as he did in the 1930s. But saying he could no longer understand the meanings of what he saw means, I think, that he gave up trying to understand. He may have been tired after the enormous works he had accomplished in the 1930s, or he may have been dismayed at the rate of change in the country. But whatever the reason, he gave up looking and listening and trying to make connections between what he saw and heard. For the sake of one's art, one needs to resist the urge to cease struggling to understand the world.

EXPERIENCE AND REGIONALISM

The matter of observation is significant for regionalists and was championed in the 1920s by *The Midland*, a nationally recognized advocate of regionalism. Its editor, John T. Frederick, argued forcefully on the writer's need to know the details of the region about which he writes. In a review of Fannie Hurst's novel, *A President is Born*, Frederick chided Hurst for her inaccuracies. "It is a surprising middle western farm in that it has 'stone hedges, most of them with their top row of boulders whitewashed. . . .' It is a farm where, coevally with the electrically lighted barns, the hay is cut with a scythe. It is a farm on which late in 'the most backward spring of many a year,' the sumach is 'red as fire'; a well-managed farm, the admiration of the countryside, on which the lambs are born in October. . . ."

In *A Handbook for Short Story Writing*, Frederick wrote that: ". . . human experience is always definitely related to physical environment, is actually influenced or determined by it. In transferring the experience, then, fullness of reality can be attained only by adequate inclusion of that physical environment."

The problem with writing like Hurst's, Frederick seems to be saying, is that if the writer gets the details wrong, she is probably going to get the human experience wrong. This, mind you, applies to realism, not to works like Shakespeare's, where place is usually irrelevant. For example, it makes no difference whether *Twelfth Night* occurs on the non-existent "seacoast of Bohemia" or on a real coast. In Shakespeare's work, not even in his histories, is character dependent on place.

In regional writing the details are significant. According to Frederick, Ms. Hurst attempts to convince us of the reality of her story by adding local color, but gets the details wrong. By getting the details wrong she reveals she has no knowledge of how physical conditions affected the culture she attempted to portray. But a culture is what a people make and therefore an expression of their character. Hurst knows neither the physical conditions nor the culture.

Put in positive terms, a great work of realism gives us the sense that the author has observed his subject closely. The work may be a novel, play, or poem, but the author has authority, and this authority comes in part from something closely observed, whether a person, landscape, or activity. Some writers, such as Sinclair Lewis or Émile Zola, conduct minute investigations into the subjects they write about, live in the locale of the novel, enter into the life of its people, and keep notebooks.

Details of a culture include the people's dialect, and observing a people means listening to their speech. Whether you are writing a realistic story or a Brechtian epic play, the rhythms of the writing must reflect contemporary rhythms if the work is to succeed in grabbing an audience. If you intend to write realism, it is even more imperative that you mimic varieties of speech and dialect. Even Shakespeare varied between the metaphoric and rhythmic speech of his aristocratic characters and the earthy speech of his commoners.

Writing realism entails having extensive knowledge of your subjects, which includes knowing tools and processes that are relevant to their lives. Regionalist painter Grant Wood was extremely knowledgeable about the things he painted: the shape and structure of this or that plow, the coloring and feathers of a particular breed of chicken, the harness of work horses, the anatomy

Observation 35

of a horse, and so on. If he was setting a painting in the past, he would research the details to get them right. This, combined with his technical handling of paint and the vision inspiring his work, gave his paintings authority. This is the kind of knowledge you need, and the kind you cannot fake.

EDITING YOUR SKETCHES
Just as a painter keeps sketchbooks as a source for paintings, the writer should keep collections of verbal sketches to use in other works. Sketches can have beauty, and should be saved for their own sake. After writing several dozen, start to rework them in minor ways. Polishing them is good editing practice; besides, a collection of sketches can make interesting reading, especially if unified by subject or theme. In editing and rewriting, however, beware of cutting some of your best spontaneous work.

The following pieces are three versions of a sketch done one afternoon in La Crosse, Wisconsin. The workshop writers were told to go onto the streets and into various businesses to make sketches and records of conversations that, when assembled, would give a kaleidoscopic vision of downtown La Crosse. Each student was asked to write two kinds of sketches: a still life and an activity. The still life might be a window display, a back alley, or an empty construction site. The activity could be any human interaction whatsoever.

This sketch was written after the group had read selections from *Cathay*, a small collection of Chinese and Japanese poems translated by Ezra Pound. Pound's renderings, which are models of sharp imagery and concision, greatly impressed workshop writer, Ron Kittleson. I have included the three drafts of one of his sketches to see what was gained and lost in the process.

> First draft:
> Dark corner illuminated by beer sign behind the old man sits staring shaking breathing jagged cold tubes to his nostrils breathes again and swears at his opponent the computer—
> His fingers curled and unsteady bony he breathes again and asks demands a glass of orange juice and peanuts— The

jukebox abruptly blares drowning out the understanding and subdues the air—thick old darkness surrounds him

Second draft:
Dark corner illuminates the man a beer sign behind him he sits and stares his hands shake his breath jagged cold tubes to his nostrils he breathes again and swears at his opponent the video game. His fingers bony stiff he breathes again and beckons for a glass of orange juice.

Third draft:
Dark corner illuminates the man beer sign behind him he sits and stares his hands shakes his breath jagged cold tubes to his nostrils he breathes again and swears at his opponent the computer screen— His fingers bony stiff he breathes again and beckons for a glass of orange juice.

Note the differences between all three drafts. If I were to print one of them in an anthology, I would select the second. It is concise, it moves rapidly, it has a sense of drama.
For all observation exercises, carry a small notebook that can be kept in a purse or pocket.

Exercise
Pick three of your sketches and rework them until you think they are finished. After you revise them, put them aside for several days, then review your first and final drafts to see what has been gained or lost in the process. If you are doing these exercises with a group or class, give one another feedback.

SKETCHING AS THE BASIS FOR PROSE POEMS

Sketches can be used as the basis for prose poems and stories. One of my favorite prose poets, El Gilbert, has spent many years in Nashville, studying people in public places, usually coffee shops or restaurants where she can sit for hours smoking cigarettes and writing. She uses her notes and sketches as the basis for many of her poems. Gilbert participated in the Nashville writing workshop when it contained an exciting mix of homeless and non-homeless writers. She is a great observer who has lived in at least a dozen cities and small towns from Port Arthur, Texas to New York and Los Angeles and points between.

The following work, "Holes in the Wall," is typical of her observation poems. It begins with a description of the setting, the person, and event which catch her attention. These trigger thoughts and associations, which eventually lead back to a description of the people and event. In this poem Gilbert has gone beyond observing to project thoughts and feelings onto the objects of her observation.

> 6:30 a.m. Four men sitting in the Bowery bent over coffee cups. Their clothes are remnants from Goodwill, their dreams dregs of former dreams discarded in the game of getting or trying to get.
>
> They glance up as a construction worker comes in out of the cold, orders a container of coffee to go. They stare at his back, wonder about him, how much money he has and where it is hidden: in the shoes, pants, jacket, or all three.
>
> The black man behind the counter is a drifter or disentangled dissenter who will be moving on as the tides rise and ravens begin to perch on his shoulder and he can't find a better job because his references aren't good enough.
>
> Two girls at the back table tease him about his body. He flushes/pretends not to notice as he clears dirty dishes and looks for stray coins on the floor. Nobody tips here.
>
> Nashville, late February, lower Broad or Broadway, the Times' Square section where the games are always the same and everyone looks alike.

The next prose poem, "Past Midnight," also by Gilbert, has bits of observations made on the spot, scattered throughout. It is

38 THE WRITER WITHIN

a meditation inspired by Huey's Smokehouse in Nashville, which she used to frequent. Gilbert is the woman in the poem working on her novel, the man writing philosophical essays is a friend.

> She sits in the back booth,
> works on her novel.
> He sits in the front booth,
> works on philosophical essays.
>
> It is Friday night, Music City,
> Huey's Smokehouse, formerly the Burger Boy
> where Waylon used to play pinball far into the night
> and all the waitresses carried guns in their bras.
>
> Waylon doesn't come around anymore,
> but most of the songwriters who congregate here
> don't know it, wait half of the night for a
> glimpse of the outlaw who walks through town
> unrecognized, balances the line between
> heaven and hell, hangs the moon, looks for
> an opening in the sky.
>
> A woman near the cash register says
> it's a disgrace about all the drugs in Nashville,
> orders another beer.
>
> A man at the end of the counter has a whole bag of
> African Gold in his hip pocket, orders another
> cup of coffee.
>
> Friday night, Nashville, glitter greased roadway
> rung dry, runover and put down by
> longshore sophisticates,
> big city bummers.

There are no rules one can follow to create a poem; one must learn the process by absorbing poetry and by practice. Nevertheless, it may help in writing your own prose poems to see how Gilbert has organized four of the six paragraphs or stanzas of this one. As you read the piece aloud, you will note that it is the repetition of structure of the four stanzas which helps differentiate this from ordinary prose. Gilbert's favorite poets are Carl Sandburg and Charles Bukowski and there are echoes of both in her work. If you don't know their work, read some. It will help you get a feel for this type of poem.

Exercises
1. *Identify the structure which the four sentences have in common. What other devices in the two poems helps distinguish them from prose?*
2. *Read selections from Sandburg's Chicago Poems, particularly "Mag," "Onion Days," "Mamie," "Working Girls," and "To a Contemporary Bunkshooter."*
3. *Take one of your sketches and transform it into a prose poem.*

PORTRAITS OF PEOPLE

The easiest portrait to write is a sketch of someone you have known for years. Begin by either telling someone about this person, or by making notes on his appearance, gestures, habits, speech, and so on. Here is one written by Murray Hudson for his book, *Dirt & Duty*, published by Free River Press. The character, Herman Ozmont, was a farmhand employed by Hudson.

> Herman "Son" Ozmont was a true character. He made up phrases and terms on the spot or adapted them from his country sayings. Things that went quickly were "as fast as a cat can lick its ass," or "quick as a dose of salts through a widow woman." Big rains were "chunk movers" or "frog stranglers." Since he couldn't read, he confused words wildly: "propaganda" became "a bunch of Proctor and Gamble."
> Herman was brave but superstitious. He believed in ghosts. Dad once sneaked up to the cabin where Herman was taking a shower. He made a high pitched "ooh" sound and scratched on the screen. Herman ran out with tee shirt

and shorts on, shoes in hand, jumped in his blue pickup and scattered gravel all the way around Palestine Cemetery.

Herman loved life: farming, women, booze, music, dancing, and making people laugh. Not necessarily in that order.

He was a twelve-year old boy in a pot-bellied, middle-aged body. The grin came from the kid inside him, and it was catching. He had a natural attraction for dirt and grease. "I ought to come down to the shop first thing in the morning and jump in the used oil barrel," he commented on this get down and dirty quality.

But he got slicked up on the weekends when he was going out with the gals. He'd smooth some Grecian Formula into his wavy gray hair and take off five years. And, if he was drinking, he would douse himself with Old Spice.

I had no trouble knowing when he was working on a toot, because the after shave was a dead giveaway within a range of fifty feet. Here Son would come with his country khakis, western shirt with vee pocket flaps and red roses that matched his scrubbed and beer-inspired complexion. He would put his hand on my shoulder and tell me how much he dearly loved to farm, which he did.

Herman was the kind of person who was both the bane and pleasure of my farming career. I spent more time with him than any other person I worked with, for almost a dozen years, and I grew to both love and loathe the man. It is a plain case of Jekyll and Hyde: when he was sober, Son was jovial, bouncy, eager to do anything, and a pleasure to work with. When he was drinking he stunk, he lied, he cracked up cars, he womanized, he did all the things that made me try to get him to go to AA. But even though he admitted after some binges, "I guess I must be a real alkyhaulic," still it didn't deter him from cranking up the blue Chevy pickup we provided him and sneaking off down to Louise's Cafe where anyone could buy beer anytime on the Siberian fringe of Dyer County. Then he would toodle the mile or so back to the brick veneer farmhand house and lock himself in and drink the six pack or two, and, as he got progressively

worse, live like a pig in a sty.
We finally had to move him out to a trailer house. He looked so pathetic, like a dog that knows he deserved the whipping for sucking eggs, but still evokes pity in the whipper. He had hidden beer in the dresser behind his socks and swore that he didn't have any. Dad discovered the warm six-pack as we moved the dresser. Herman had the most childish hang head look. He died a few days later.
Herman was our mechanic, my right hand man and good friend. His death made it more obvious than ever that the farming operation was dying, too.
Years later I still see that jack-o-lantern smile as he cracked a joke.

Here is another portrait, but one integrated into the story line, and written for another autobiography, *A Rogues Island Memoir*, published by Free River Press. The author, Rod Haynes, is reflecting on a time after high school when he worked in a food warehouse.

The main foreman running the floor where the truck orders were filled was named Albert. He was a high school graduate with stringy, greasy hair who spent a substantial amount of his time directly in my face, yelling at high volume. For whatever reason, I was never much intimidated by him, which no doubt annoyed him. Albert weighed at least 270 pounds, wore size 15 shoes, and had this annoying habit of flinging his hair off to one side whenever it fell down over his face, which was often. When Albert spoke to a crew member, he always stared off to one side, rarely looking the person straight in the eye. Even at the age of 17, I thought his effectiveness as a leader on the floor of the warehouse was greatly diminished because of his reluctance to issue direct orders while maintaining eye-to-eye contact with his subordinates. It wasn't good because you didn't get the sense Albert was secure with himself. I mean, who the hell was in charge here?

Albert hated the fact that I planned to go on to college, that my entire future wasn't wrapped up in plans to work at Imperial Imports for the next two decades. So he started in on harassing me from the first day I reported there. I had the idea he wanted me to know college wasn't the only road to success; after all, look where he was.

I looked and was doubly determined to go on to college.

Ensuring eight sixteen-ounce jars of pickled onion packed in a slippery cardboard box four tiers above ground level made it all the way down to the floor intact, especially when you were working solo on a cold November morning, wasn't easy. When accidents took place, as they invariably did, the noise and resulting mess on the floor was spectacular. It was also embarrassing. Usually these incidents brought Albert running to the scene, spluttering obscenities and threats, kicking at the air with his leather boots, and throwing a mop in my direction, telling me to "get it picked up you dumb shit."

Like the other portraits Rod Haynes wrote for his book, Albert's profile is integrated into the action, and reflects the fact that his memoir, although written as a series of short stories, follows a continuous narrative thread. Murray Hudson's memoir does not. Most of his stories and reflections are discrete units that seldom have any narrative relation to the others.

Exercises
1. *For the best results, this exercise should be done with a group. Begin by having someone read the description of Herman Ozmont aloud awhile the others listen. Then have someone ask questions. Recall what Herman looked like when working, and when he was about to go "on the town." Why does Hudson refer to him as "Jekyll and Hyde"? What were some of Herman's qualities that Hudson liked? What were some he disliked? Recall some of the peculiarities of Herman's speech. Recall whatever you can. Repeat the process for Albert, recalling his physical appearance, his*

peculiarities, his relation to the young man.
2. *Pick some character you have known, and if you are a member of a writers' group or class, tell the group about this person. If the group has questions about the person, they should ask. This will help you explore other facets of this character. Now write a sketch of him. Keep in mind his physical appearance, speech, actions, and idiosyncrasies. Read the sketch to the group. Have them tell you what they liked and what they want to know more about. Have them tell you if there was anything in the telling that you omitted from the writing. Add it.*

FICTIONAL ACCOUNTS OF REAL PEOPLE

After writing a portrait of someone you have known, make a few transformations—change the person's name and residence, and perhaps his occupation or physical characteristics—and put them in a story of your invention. What counts is preserving the person's character, which is demonstrated by what he does and says.

Murray Hudson's father, Jack Hudson, wrote a few stories on the Mississippi Delta that he expanded into a book of memoirs, *Feedin', Fishin', Fightin' & Farmin'*, beginning with his days on his grandparents' farm during the Depression. As a youngster his best friend was a black boy, Dill, who figures in many of the stories. Like many Southerners of his generation, Mr. Hudson is a gifted story teller, and many of the anecdotes in his memoirs were based on real events and were stories he had told over the years. Many more, I discovered later, were fiction.

Since he knew his characters, and had thought about them for years, inventing stories about them was no problem. The following boyhood story combines fact with fiction.

Miss Lizzy and the Catfish
Luther Smith lived by himself on the river bank. He made his living fishing and trapping. Old Luke, that is what most people called him. Luke would find hollow cypress logs. He would float them into shallow water next to a deep hole. He would chop a hole in a log next to the bank. He called

that his peep hole. He would leave the big end open next to the deep water. The big catfish liked to nest in the log. They would go in to lay [deposit] their eggs. One day I was fishing at the deep hole. I saw old Luke floating a log into the bank. He didn't see me, if he had he would not have stopped there. I stayed real still until he was gone. Old Dan my bull dog was sitting next to me. I put my hand over his mouth so he could not bark.

About two weeks later, when I went fishing again, I decided to check old Luke's log. When I looked in I saw the largest catfish I had ever seen. I eased away, I didn't want to scare it. When I got home I went down to Dill's house. I told him that I had seen a catfish in Old Luke's log that would way 50 lbs. It had started raining so we couldn't work in the cotton next day. I told Dill to get a 9 ft. pick sack and we would stretch it over the open end of the log. He could hold the sack and I would take a stick and punch the fish and run it in to the sack.

We carried a plow line to tie onto the pick sack. We then tied the rope to a bush by the log. When I punched the catfish the log exploded. When it hit the end of the sack it jerked Dill into the water. All I could see was Dill's feet, the fish was headed for deep water. I ran back to the bush and got a hold on the rope. I was able to pull the fish and Dill back to shallow water. I asked Dill why he didn't turn the sack loose, he said he didn't have time, when the fish hit the end of the sack, it was just like a bull.

We both got hold of the rope and pulled the fish out on the bank. We opened the sack and looked in. It was one big catfish. . . .

[The boys put the fish in the sack and tie one end of the sack to their horse and head for home.]

It was about two miles from home. We decided to give the fish a drink. We pulled the fish into the water and were standing with the rope in our hand. We heard someone up on the bridge holler "What are you doing down there?" It was Old Man Bob Hoagy. We told him we had caught a big cat fish and there was another one still in the water. He came sliding down the bank and looked in the sack. He let out a yell that sounded like an Indian. He said "did you say that you saw another one like that in the hole?" We said yes we think it was larger, but don't tell anyone we are going to try to catch it tomorrow.

Old Man Bob always knew everything. Miss Lizzy was his wife. Old Man Bob and Miss Lizzy had a 30A (acre) farm on a back road. . . .

Old Man Bob climbed the bank and took off in a run. . . . He went to the barn and got four broken sacks. He unraveled them, sewed them together and made a seine. . . He hitched his mules to the wagon, put the seine in the wagon.

He went in the house to get Miss Lizzy. Miss Lizzy wasn't ready. . . . He hollered at Miss Lizzy to hurry up. If we don't get that catfish this evening, Jack and Dill will get it early in the morning. Miss Lizzy put on her high top shoes and got in the wagon.

When they got to the creek, Old Bob helped Lizzy slide down the creek bank. He went back to the wagon and got the seine. He slid down the creek bank and unrolled the seine. He gave one stick that the seine was tied to to Lizzy and said for her to walk along the bank. He waded across the creek. . . .

[Miss Lizzy slid into the river.]

The mail carrier was crossing the bridge about this time. He heard all of the noise under the bridge. He got out of his car and looked under the bridge. Ben Smith was the mailman. When he saw the shape Miss Lizzy was in he called to her to stand still. He got a long pole and slid down the bank. Miss Lizzy got one end of the pole and Ben Smith pulled Miss Lizzy back up the bank. Miss Lizzy was muddy from head to foot she had so much mud on her face she could hardly open her eyes. Old Bob crawled up the bank with the seine. Ben Smith asked Bob what are you doing seining the creek. Bob told him about the big catfish that Jack and Dill had caught in the creek. Ben Smith said "Hell, Bob, those boys were pulling your leg. They didn't catch that fish in the creek." Bob helped Miss Lizzy into the wagon. The last thing Ben heard, Miss Lizzy was giving Old Bob hell. By the time Ben Smith finished his mail route, everyone had heard about Old Bob and the big catfish. . . .

[After Old Bob left to get Miss Lizzy] I told Dill to get on the horse and go home. I said for him to get [my uncle] Leo to bring the T-Ford. I would stay with the fish. In about 1 hour Leo and Dill arrived in the T-Ford. We loaded the catfish in the back of the Ford. Dill got on the mule and we all left for home. When we got home we got the cotton scales, we got some bailing wire, tied the scales to the rafters in the car shed. Josh [Dill's daddy] and Leo tied the cotton sack to the cotton scale. To way the fish. It weighted 56 lbs. After the fish was cleaned we had 2 dish pans full of cat fish stakes.

Even though Mr. Hudson was not present when Bob Hoagy arrived back home to get Miss Lizzy, he talks as though he were an eyewitness. That's the signal that this part is fiction. What other part or parts do you think were invented?

Exercises:
1. *Write a portrait of one of the people you have observed. If you have overhead snatches of the person's conversation, write a two page sketch or portrait of that person.*
2. *Write a short story about a group of people, perhaps ones whom you have watched in a coffee shop, an auto shop, a police station.*

FICTIONAL PORTRAITS
Sherwood Anderson's *Winesburg, Ohio* is a collection of stories

about people in a small town inspired by Clyde, Ohio, where Anderson grew up. The stories are united not only by location, but by the recurrence of characters. Perhaps a third of all of the characters are impelled to speak to George Willard, the young reporter on the *Winesburg Eagle*. Almost all are lonely, trapped inside themselves, trying to communicate to Willard the one truth each believes he has discovered. Their stories remind us of Thoreau's claim that "the mass of men lead lives of quiet desperation."

Anderson's book offers an excellent model for emulation. It is a collection of portraits, which, as Hemingway wrote, "were simply written and sometimes beautifully written and he knew the people he was writing about and cared deeply for them." That he cared deeply for them is clearly evident. Some were based on people he knew, others grew out of his imagination, stimulated by faces that he saw on city streets, in restaurants and cafés, anywhere. No matter where you live, in the country, in a small town or big city, try Anderson's experiment and begin thinking about people whom you observe fleetingly.

Stand at a busy intersection or anywhere people mill. Find an interesting person. Watch him. Take notes. If he goes into stores or restaurants, follow him. Discover what you can.

People with marked mannerisms are easiest to study. If you can observe someone for an extended period, watch for gestures. Do they have one when tired? When angry? When frustrated? What are their public gestures? What are their private gestures when they think they are not observed?

Bus stations and restaurants in the pre-dawn hours are good places to find characters. Many writers have had a fascination with the night and studied its denizens. Thomas Wolfe began a strange literary experiment called *The Hound of Darkness*, which was a portrait of America at night. The work, never completed, was to consist of a series of unrelated events across the country occurring on the same night. Kerouac, who was a great admirer of Wolfe, was also fascinated by what he referred to as "the American Night."

Study night people. Go to a restaurant at five a.m. when the last of the nighthawks are about to leave and the morning shift and customers are about to enter. The restaurant will be nearly empty. Sit until the conversations start. Look at the faces. What do they tell you? What do their clothes suggest? At five-thirty the regulars began coming in, a few at a time. Why did they come here so early? Are they waiting for the morning shift at the plant?

Go to a bus station and observe. Where is the poorly dressed old woman with the suitcase going? To see her sister? Daughter? Son? Why is she going? Is there a problem in the family? What about the young man and woman, leaning on each other, asleep? Study their faces. What stories do their faces tell?

As you observe your neighborhood or town, make a list of the people who strike you forcefully, especially those you see regularly. In our area we have a neighboring farmer whose mother, now dead, wanted him to be a girl and dressed him as one. Years later, when a ladies' card club met at their farmhouse, the boy and his father came in from the fields but, too embarrassed to walk in the front door and meet the women, they climbed a ladder to the second story. To this day the son, now a middle-aged man, dresses in woman's clothes—black hose or tights, short skirt, blouse or T-shirt, and bra—even when doing field work. He is not derided by his neighbors and is seldom mentioned in conversation. He lives with his father, and goes to town early in the morning to sell eggs at the grocery. Think of how lonely he must be.

This farmer would have been a character for Sherwood Anderson. But so too would very quiet people who conform. Pick a few who interest you and begin to understand why they made the choices they have. How do you think they feel about those choices? Ask yourself, "What did they want when they were young, and what have they got now? How do they feel about themselves?" Think about these things and you will begin to discover their relations with others. As you give dramatic form to those relations you will begin to create a world.

OBSERVING PLACES

Apply the same kind of concentration to place that you have to people. Find a place to become intimate with, one that you will return to time after time.

When El Gilbert was a member of the Nashville writing workshop, she and another workshop member were living with an elderly couple that had given them a room. I asked El, who had been an executive secretary in New York City, to write her autobiography. At this juncture of her story, she suddenly found herself without an apartment and in need of a place to stay. She begins:

> Now where? Certainly not the Rescue Mission or the Salvation Army . . . & those were the only feasible choices in a city that was often cited as the music capitol of the world, a city swelling rapidly to a million in population, a city where shelters & rehabilitation centers for single women didn't exist.
>
> Having no options open to me, I contacted Abbey & George Schmidt, a middle-aged couple I had known a few years, who always told me I could stay with them if worse came to worse. It had.
>
> They agreed to take me in for a while even though they were cramped for space. Well . . . What else was new? Everywhere I went there seemed to be some kind of space problem. No room in the inn, to be more explicit.
>
> Their house was a two-bedroom stone structure on a hill convenient to nothing for those without cars or adequate means of transportation. I shuddered to think of walking in this neighborhood late at night. The streets were dark, winding roads overgrown with thick trees & heavy brush, a perfect setting for muggers, rapists & murderers.
>
> From the street the dwelling resembled something out of a Ray Bradbury novel or a Dracula movie. On the inside it looked as though a whirlwind had blown through it, depositing a huge can of garbage in the process. I stared in disbelief. There was litter on every chair, table & inch of floor. Dirty dishes were piled in the kitchen sink. Half-empty cartons of food could be seen amid a collection of tools & filthy clothes on a small work area. Garbage surfaced in a restaurant-sized trash barrel. Water & urine were all over the bathroom floor. I doubted that it had ever been mopped.

A shower curtain hung by shreds from a single hook over the bathtub, which was completely corroded. Towel fixtures were broken off from the wall. Blackened towels & soiled articles of underwear were balled in corners. The living room rugs reeked. Dust covered everything. The door of the hall linen closet was ajar, revealing a jumbled mess of sheets & pillowcases. Abbey & George's bedroom was a nightmare, complete with open milk bottles, which were used as urinals during the night & not emptied until they were filled . . . if then. The only air conditioner was in this room, but it was put on very sparingly. The windows were painted shut. The screws on both the front & back doors were ripped & torn beyond repair. These doors were locked most of the time, adding to the general stuffiness of the atmosphere. A side porch enclosed by rotting screens served as a living room in warm months, permitting an army of flies access to the rest of the house.

A medium-sized rusty-colored female dog named Bruno ran in & out of the debris, using any clear floor space as a bathroom. Approximately six months old, she had not been licensed or ever taken to a vet. Abbey & George said they didn't have the money. Neighbors threatened to call the dog catcher if they saw the dog running loose. To avoid this, George kept her indoors nearly all of the time, making no effort to paper train her. Her diet was the cheapest dry dog food they could find.

At first I thought the overwhelming odor in the house was the dog. Then I realized it was far more than that, but just what it was impossible to pinpoint.

Exercise
Using Gilbert's introduction, write a story about George and Abbey.

For there to be a story, something has to happen. What is it? Is it precipitated by the dog, by the house guests, or by someone from the outside?

Let the story write itself. Don't plot it out. Just think about what kind of people George and Abbey are. Why do they let people stay with them? Are they getting something in exchange? Your story may be comic, it may be pathetic. Don't make any prior determinations. Just write.

SOUND

Sound, like visuals, can help create a sense of place or set the stage for an activity. Here, for example, is a brief description by Murray Hudson of a time when he and a group of women were hoeing weeds in a cotton field.

> Ordinarily I heard a constant chatter at my back, like a flock of chickens. I believe they all talked at once, at least some of the time. One July day about noon when the temperature shot above a hundred degrees, we were in the half-mile long rows on the east side of the Oil Barn field and were nearing the end when I sensed something strange, no noise from my choppers. I looked back, and one of the younger girls was flat on the ground. The others were gathering around her, fanning and shading her. I asked the mother and another grown woman to take her out to the end, get her a drink of cool water and sit her in the shade. I realized it was too hot to chop at midday, so we cut out the three hottest hours of the day and chopped later in the evening. I had never been around anyone with heat stroke, and I didn't want to start now.

When Hudson likens the sounds of woman chattering to "a flock of chickens" I can hear them. His first sentence also gives me a picture: Hudson is in front, his back to the women. I picture them moving slowly through adjacent rows, heads down, chopping and talking. It readies us for the action which follows.

Sound can be used to create a sense of place. Here, for example, is a paragraph from *Maggie: A Girl of the Streets*, a novella by nineteenth-century American writer Stephen Crane. *Maggie* is set in New York's Bowery, then a district of slum tenements.

> Jimmie and the old woman listened in the hall. Above the

muffled roar of conversation, the dismal wailings of babies at night, the thumping of feet in unseen corridors and rooms, and the sound of varied hoarse shoutings in the street, and the rattling of wheels over cobbles, they heard the screams of the child and the roars of the mother die away to a feeble moaning and a subdued bass muttering.

Every time Crane mentions a sound, we hear it. In this scene he layers sound upon sound, so that after giving us the first—"the muffled roar of conversation"— he gives us a second, "the dismal wailings of babies." With the first sound still in our heads we are given the second. Then a third, a fourth, a fifth and finally a sixth sound, which is that of a screaming child and roaring mother. We hear sounds in the tenement and outside of it, and finally we hear six all together, and in our head is the very first image of the paragraph: the little boy and the old woman listening. If you read the story, you will know that what they are listening to is the very last sound, for the little baby is Jimmie's brother. Crane knowingly gives us this sound last.

If he had started the list with the mother and baby, who are the most important element in the scene, he would have destroyed the drama by drowning them out with the other sounds. Instead, he builds tension that leads to the mother and child, beginning with the sight of the boy and old woman listening. But as every effective scene has a final diminution of tension before its end, here, in this mini-scene, the sound of baby and mother "die away."

The very first paragraph of *Maggie* gives us a description of life on the street which relies not only on visuals for its power, but sound. The book opens with a stone fight between young boys, and is a metaphor for Bowery life, a struggle in which only the fittest survive the jungle of the streets.

A very little boy stood upon a heap of gravel for the honor of Rum Alley. He was throwing stones at howling urchins from Devil's Row, who were circling about the heap and pelting him. His infantile countenance was livid with the fury of battle. His small body was writhing in the delivery

Observation 53

of oaths.

"Run, Jimmie, run! Dey'll git yeahs!" screamed a retreating Rum Alley child.

"Naw," responded Jimmie with a valiant roar, "dese mugs can't make me run."

Howls of renewed wrath went up from Devil's Row throats. Tattered gamins on the right made a furious assault on the gravel heap. On their small, convulsed faces shone the grins of true assasins. As they charged, they threw stones and cursed in shrill chorus.

The urchins howl, the little boy roars oaths in return. His last ally retreats and screams for him to run. Then, finally, the urchins curse in shrill chorus as they charge their enemy. Sounds and visuals are effectively integrated: every action is accompanied by a sound.

Exercises
1. *Write a short scene which begins with a sound that indicates an activity. Make that activity an important element within the scene.*
2. *Write a short scene which layers sounds on one another. Use the sounds to create tension.*
3. *Write a short action scene in which sound and visuals are integrated throughout.*

CHAPTER FOUR
GENESIS & METAMORPHOSIS

INTERNAL COMPOSITION v. WRITE AND REWRITE
As you probably have discovered, writing can be both exhilarating and frustrating. You may have experienced the occasional poem or story writing itself, but if you have worked at writing, you usually find yourself revising until you get it right.

How is it then that there are writers who seem to get it right, most of the time, in the first draft? Thomas Nashe, a gifted Elizabethan pamphleteer, playwright, satirist, and word juggler, boasted that he 'wrote as fast as his hand could trot.' My hunch is that Nashe worked out his writings in his head before committing them to paper.

This points to two methods of writing. One is the common method of writing and rewriting, in which we put down draft after draft, rearranging paragraphs and rewriting sentences. The process may begin with a sketchy outline, which is used to suggest rather than dictate content. By using an outline as a tentative skeleton rather than as a straitjacket, you allow yourself to integrate the discoveries you make as you proceed.

The other method is to think the work out in one's head before committing words to paper. Internal composition can involve a variety of methods. It may mean telling the story or explaining the idea to others. It may involve rearranging the parts of the work in one's head to see which order works best. It may involve visualizing the action. Or it may involve some self-induced, quasi-dream state in which the writer allows the unconscious to play a role in gestation. When I began writing, I used the write and rewrite method not only to polish drafts but to help discover what it was I wanted to say. The older I get, however, the more I find myself using the method of internal composition, even to the point where I talk out the essay or story in my head.

TELLING & RETELLING

We looked at storytelling in the chapter on strategies, but now are going to reexamine it from the point of view of expanding and refining one's story or essay. The best instance I have seen of the success of this method was a personal essay by Bill Welsh, a member of the northeast Iowa farm writing workshop. Bill joined the workshop primarily to spread the gospel of organic farming. He decided that the story of how and why he went organic would be the first piece he would write. For years he had been telling this story to farmers at conferences, and when he came to write it, completed his first draft in one evening. It was not only well-structured but firmly worded, with little need of revision.

When we tell the same story over and over, as Bill did, we eventually finalize it, and for ever after our tellings remain virtually identical. I first encountered this habit when I interviewed and later became friends with a famous jazz musician. He was an elderly man with a repertoire of two or three dozen stories that he told and retold. I taped and transcribed some of them, and later read articles about him written years before. I noticed that he had told other journalists the stories he was telling me, and that the wordings of the different versions were almost identical. A few years later I noticed the same practice with others who repeated stories. It became clear that when you tell a story numerous times you try to find the best wording for it, and in so doing put it into fixed form.

Exercise
Think of someone who has meant a lot to you. Pick a crucial moment in your relationship with her and tell it to someone. Talk about the difference this person made in your life. If unusual or striking, describe her habits, looks, and gestures.
   Even if storytelling is difficult for you, force yourself to do this exercise. You may think the listener is uninterested; persevere

just the same. Then think of details you omitted from the story. Tell it to someone else and include them. The more you tell the story, the more comfortable you will become with it.

TALKING OUT AN ESSAY

The method outlined in this section works best for an argumentative or persuasive essay, especially when you are knowledgeable and passionate about your subject. It involves visualizing an audience—it may be an audience of one—and talking directly to it. It involves histrionics, presenting your ideas dramatically, with gestures, and by raising and lowering your voice. All this is done internally, inside your head.

This procedure does two things. First, sentences and paragraphs emerge; second, the drama of your presentation will carry over into your writing.

But before beginning the "presentation," you have to examine the subject in your mind, considering as many aspects as occur to you. At this point don't decide which aspects are relevant, just accept all topics that suggest themselves. Then pretend you are talking to your audience, explain your thesis and the reasons for it. As sentences and even paragraphs emerge, repeat them in your mind. Go on to new topics. More ideas will emerge, including connections between the parts. Keep in mind that you are not trying to generate the entire essay, just the highlights. Let the subject percolate in your mind until it creates an uncomfortable pressure; then begin to write. By letting pressure build you will generate a lot of words very quickly.

The next step is trying to decide the most effective arrangement of the parts.

When you have committed all your thoughts to paper, read them and begin cutting irrelevant and tangential material. It may take several readings to decide to let go of an important but inessential idea. Once the irrelevancies are eliminated, the relation of the parts will emerge quite naturally. For example, when you see arguments for a proposition or idea scattered throughout your notes, pull them together into contiguous paragraphs. Do the same for other propositions and ideas. By doing this you will create several sections, each arguing for or explaining a distinct proposition. Begin editing and expanding the sections. As you do so, it will become clear how to arrange them. If you have not had formal training in composition, rely upon your acquired, informal knowledge of argument and demonstration to help you think and feel your way.

In Roman times writers and rhetoricians had definite outlines to follow. The two most famous writers of Roman manuals were Cicero and Quintillian, whose treatises on the subject became the basis for our college composition classes. Quintillian wrote: "No art is ever born at once. We clear fields, we tame animals, what is most natural is what nature permits to be brought to perfection. How can style without structure be stronger than one welded together and well arranged? . . . Style is better flowing in ordered channels, not like a wild river; for beauty always accompanies art. . . In my opinion artistic structure gives force and direction to our thoughts."

For centuries, even into the Reformation, the outline of arguments and demonstrations, such as the one that Erasmus used for *In Praise of Folly,* followed classic rhetorical structure with its various divisions. Today little of that outline remains in college classrooms, yet essayists are still writing powerful pieces. Part of that is due to the fact that we are still reading older works in which classical techniques for argument and persuasion are present. Besides, certain rhetorical techniques are natural expressions of the mind. We don't need text books to tell us that a proposition is stronger when backed by examples than when it remains an unsubstantiated claim. And we seem to know instinctively that there is a strength in an argument which presents a thesis and its antithesis, and uses this opposition to establish the strength of one claim and the weakness of the other, point by point. A study of a good rhetoric manual will strengthen your instinctive knowledge of these and other practices.

Exercise
Once you have gotten an idea for an essay, begin to improvise it aloud or in your head. Imagine an audience of one or more per

sons to whom you are speaking. See how much you can create before writing it.

THE STORY AS INTERNAL MOVIE

Almost invariably before I begin writing a narrative I run events over in my mind, visualizing the characters and action in a kind of internal movie. This is good for writing detailed oriented realism. It involves visualizing the characters' facial features, gestures, size, and physical peculiarities, the objects in the environment, the sounds, and the condition of the light. This method is akin to that of the artist or artisan in preindustrial societies who would envision the finished piece before beginning work.

You can begin your visualization by imagining an activity, a place, or people. In *Improvisation for the Theater,* Viola Spolin used these three fundamental aspects of a scene to create games for actors. Spolin's ground-breaking work is now standard training for improvisers, and its insights into the creative process also offer writers a method for generating scenes. Spolin notes that every scene consists of a Who, a What, and a Where. In other words, every scene has at least one character, somewhere, doing something. The actor can develop her scene beginning with any one of these; the other two will develop from it.

Let us say two actors are given an activity, such as waiting for a bus. One is young and late for an appointment; the other is elderly and has no destination in mind. Each actor is assigned one of the roles. That is all. Out of their gestures and actions will come their dialogue. If the actors are skilled, the conversation will have shape and the scene will have a beginning, middle, and end.

In just the same way a writer may improvise a story, beginning with a Who, a What, or a Where. He may begin by envisioning his characters in detail, then picturing where they are and what they are doing. Or he may begin with a place or activity, and let his imagination generate the other two.

If you start with an activity, let it unfold in your mind. Pretend you are watching a movie: see the colors and forms, hear the sounds, listen to the conversations. Watch the gestures the characters make as they speak. Visualize their surroundings. As you see and hear your movie, rite it down. On this, your first draft, you are acting passively as recorder, and the process will give you a much greater richness of detail than you might otherwise achieve.

On your second draft take the role of director. Review your recorder's notes and decide what needs cutting or amplifying. Then visualize your scenes again. If a character interests you or a place or object draws your attention, follow it. As you "shoot new scenes," remember that as director you can vary shots, moving from long shot to medium shot to close-up, in any order you please. You can focus on a character's face, then move the camera down to look at his hands, feet, or stomach, whatever needs attention. You can cut a scene before the action is over, when the conclusion is obvious. You can make fast, jarring cuts between scenes. Or you can insert narration between scenes to slow the pace.

Exercise
1. *Write the close-up of an activity. Then pull the camera back and see more of it. Describe it.*
2. *Take a story that you have already written, reread it, then visualize it part by part. As you visualize a part, write it down. Repeat the process until you've satisfied yourself that you've achieved the right level of detail, then read the first and last versions to someone. Ask for reactions.*

LETTING THE UNCONSCIOUS PLAY A ROLE

If you have become bogged down in your writing, at whatever stage, set it aside. The conscious mind can only do so much. At some point the unconscious must be allowed to do its work. Taking a long walk and thinking about something is one way of dealing with writer's block or tiredness; taking a nap with the intention of allowing the unconscious to work the problem out is another. Even a state halfway between sleep and waking is a time to meditate on the problem you are trying to solve. The main point is to be aware that a good deal of our serious writing goes on subconsciously, and to allow your conscious mind the time it needs to rest and become reinvigorated by unconscious processes.

Every writer develops his own schedule. Lewis Mumford wrote for only four hours a day, yet he was one of the most respected and prolific writers of the twentieth century. He found that working a garden reinvigorated him, and that the scent of flowers sharpened his intellect. You may find yourself writing once a day between specific hours, or breaking the writing into several chunks scattered from morning to late at night.

Just because you are blocked doesn't mean you are finished for the day. You will learn to distinguish between exhaustion and writer's block. When you have written yourself out for the day you will cease to make sense. Know enough to stop. Writer's block, on the other hand, can occur even when the mind is sharp. In that case simply find another activity and let the unconscious solve the problem.

Exercise
Experiment with writing at different times of the day to find which works best for you. Practice writing for longer and longer periods. Experiment with the different suggested ways of coping with writer's block.

EXPANSION

One of the first things I notice about student writing is that descriptions of events are usually minimal. The event may have been full of drama, filled with arguments, emotions, and physical activity, but the written version is usually quite compressed.

Suppose, for example, that the writer is a high school student who has won a track event. The student might write the following account: "Six of us lined up for the race. We ran in a pack for the first two hundred yards, then one by one the others fell behind. Eventually only one runner could keep pace with me. We ran in a dead heat until the last ten yards when I pushed myself to pass the finish line, just ahead of him."

This account does not give us a feel for the effort of the race. We don't know the physical exhaustion the runner might have felt the last dozen yards, what it is like to breathe in such a case, how the legs strain, and so on. Nor do we know the feelings that the competing runner might have inspired in the writer. The account is abstract; it needs fleshing out.

This is why I have students tell their stories before writing them. It helps them relive the experience and provides the class with details. If the class wants to know more about specifics, they will ask, and the teller is encouraged to include them. But even after a telling, the student often omits details from the written version. It usually takes several rewrites before the writer includes enough specifics in the story to make it rival the telling.

Here is a sample from *A Rogues Island Memoir* in which Rod Haynes is looking back to his days thirty years ago as a caddy at a Rhode Island country club. In the first draft, his story about caddying ran twelve pages and was extremely compressed. It took four or five drafts for Haynes to expand it adequately. The total now runs twenty-four pages.

Here is a paragraph from the first version:

> A few years later, when the movie CADDY SHACK arrived in movie theaters, we were convinced that the script writers had been caddies at Kirkbrae at one time in their lives. As we matured, it became increasingly impossible for us to take many of the golfers we served seriously, although we understood we were being paid to work for them. We were present on the golf course as members were carted off in handcuffs by federal law enforcement agents for whatever crimes they were accused of. We listened to some of them brag in detail about hookers and Las Vegas and money and cars It was an education and it became even more of a comedy in time, when the children of the golfers came out onto the course and started carrying on like their parents. We dismissed the kids as being spoiled and obnoxious, and not worthy of much of our time or effort. And if they had the audacity to start bossing us around, we usually told them to go straight to hell in short order."

The paragraph is begging for expansion. When I read it, I wanted to know what some of the members had been arrested for, what some had done for the caddies to lose respect for them, and what specifically the members bragged about.

Here's what Rod did with this excerpt. As you read, keep in mind that the writer and his friend Darrell were seventh-grade students at the time.

> Darrell told me the tale of the day two FBI agents appeared out of nowhere on the second hole flashing their I.D. badges, asking one member what his name was. Once his identity was confirmed, the member was taken off in handcuffs by the agents, the golfer riding in the back of the golfcart as if he were a bag of clubs. We never confirmed what crime he was accused of, but we were impressed by the fact that the FBI found it necessary to visit Kirkbrae personally to drag one of its members off to jail.
>
> I could not help but overhear some members regularly talk in lurid detail about the money, women, and shows of Las Vegas. Apparently the mark of success at Kirkbrae was making frequent visits to Las Vegas. The more times you went out west the more successful you were, if you accepted these guys' tales about their girlfriends and gambling. But when I thought about it further I realized neither Darrell's parents nor mine ever mentioned anything about wanting to go to Vegas. It just seemed to be a big deal at Kirkbrae. What was it about Vegas that made it so great? Darrell and I didn't get it.
>
> Wads of cash were flashed around the club by members as they stood in front of the caddies and other members. Members pulled up next to the caddy bench in their new baby blue-colored Mark V Lincoln Town Cars to unload their golf clubs, and handed us two or three bucks to haul them over to the club racks where Al McQueen, the caddy master, kept a careful eye on them before assigning a caddy to carry them for the day.
>
> Over time, the male children of the golfers came out onto the course dressed like their parents, trying to boss the caddies around. It was comical watching them appear

in expensive golf clothes while we sat there dressed in jean cut-offs and dirty tee shirts. When they got on our nerves, which was often, we usually told them to go straight to hell when their parents were out of ear shot. The kids never complained to the caddymaster because he would have probably laughed at them. Some of the kids were good golfers, but they strutted around the putting green and club house as if they owned the place.

This is an excellent expansion, but I still want to know more. For example, how did the young golfers try to boss the caddies? I would like a scene with dialogue. I would also like a scene in which we heard the men with big wads of cash bragging. I know what they talked about, but I would like to hear their words.

Exercise
Take a story that you have written, one which you feel is too compact. If you are part of a class or teacherless writing group, read your piece aloud and have others tell you which parts they would like expanded. If you are not part of a group, imagine that someone else wrote your story. Which parts would you like to see expanded? Rewrite them.

CUTTING

When I taught college composition and had students read their works aloud, I would ask the rest of the class to interrupt the reader whenever his work contained a cliche or well-worn phrase. At the beginning of the semester essays and stories would be full of phrases such as "tried and true" and "better safe than sorry," and with cliches such as "Never look a gift horse in the mouth." It became a kind of game for others to shout out "Cliche!" or "Hackneyed phrase!" whenever one was read. Students enjoyed it and there were no hurt feelings, partly because no one was immune. They very quickly became sensitive to hackneyed writing and soon were able to weed it out on their own.

The problem with using well-worn phrases and cliches is that while they may bear some general resemblance to the writer's thought, they can never do so precisely. Cliched phrases and sayings avoid exact expression, which is the goal of writing.

My college students and I practiced another kind of cutting. In the search for precision they became attuned to wordiness, which is the problem of using more words than necessary to make a point. They would take a sentence such as: "Only very infrequently did she cut the grass with her lawn mower" and prune it to: "She rarely mowed her lawn." They became aware of wordiness by exchanging papers and cutting it from one another's works. With practice wordiness becomes easy to spot. As you read each of your drafts, ask yourself, "Have I said everything in as few words as possible?" You may be surprised not only at the number of unnecessary words you may have used within a sentence, but at how many times you may have rephrased the same thought within a paragraph.

Eliminating irrelevant anecdotes or stories is a harder matter, especially in a memoir, which inevitably contains episodes to which the writer is emotionally attached. I worked with one memoir writer who could create strong dramatic scenes but could not fashion the work as a whole. Her attachment to irrelevant stories prevented her from identifying interrelated episodes that would create a compelling dynamic. Several related stories that gave us an understanding of a mother/daughter relationship would be followed by recollections of grade school friends and teachers, followed by family trips to the country, followed by the story of a flood in the writer's hometown, etc. It lacked a story line and it lacked dramatic revelation of character.

Some memoirs do not have a story line and yet they form a whole because the writer is illuminating a topic, say life in a city neighborhood, and keeps revealing it from different angles, somewhat in the manner of a video camera moving about a stationary sculpture. This is the manner of *Winesburg, Ohio*, a collection of stories of small town residents which collectively present a portrait of that town. Here there is no need for a story line that collects all the individuals because many of them are unknown to one another. But the writer who is trying to explore the changing lives of a close-knit group over a number of years has to have a story line of sorts. After all, this kind of memoir is about the impact these people have had on one another, and a story line will be the yard stick to judge whether an episode is relevant or not.

Exercise
1. *Exchange papers or stories with a friend, and see how many irrelevant words you can cut from each other's works. How many cliches or hackneyed phrases can you identify?*
2. *If you are working on a novel or a memoir, identify irrelevant episodes.*

POINT OF VIEW

The third person narrator is omniscient. He knows what the characters are thinking, he knows their pasts and futures. He can write, word for word, a discussion they had with someone forty years ago. He can tell us how they felt when they graduated from college, got married, had their first child, and so on. With the first person "I," however, all you can know is what you or your imaginary narrator has seen or heard.

In the fifteen years that I have taught writing, the one revision that actually astounded me was done by a homeless man with no formal writing background beyond high school English. Wayne Leonhard, who was a member of the Nashville workshop, wrote a fine account of a cross-country hitchhiking trip he had made in the 1970s. At the time he wrote it I was using Kerouac's prose as a model in the homeless workshop. The homeless could relate to Kerouac's experiences, and his two styles—the flat prose of *On the Road* and the more convoluted style generated by his method of spontaneous composition—offered effective models. Wayne had lived many years as a transient, including years on road construction crews, and knew he would relate to *On the Road*. I loaned him a copy. He loved it, and was inspired to write a lengthy narrative about his hitchhiking trip from Minnesota to California. Later he went on to write about his adolescence.

He wrote both narratives in the first person, modeled after the sentence structure and rhythms of *On the Road*. Wayne became a very able stylist. Then one day, without preliminary announcement, he appeared at the workshop with a large chunk of his manuscript rewritten in the third person, exploring aspects of his experience that could not be done in first person. I asked where he got the idea for this revision, and he replied it was his own.

Wayne's instinct to compare first and third person accounts of the same event, to see the advantages and limitations of each, is the instinct that every writer should have. All too many of us assume that the first person account of our experiences, which is the natural account, is necessarily the better fit. Thomas Wolfe wrote his vast autobiographical saga, *Of Time and the River*, in the first person, but his publisher changed it to the third. Read a dozen pages of that novel and convert two or three paragraphs to the first person. See what you think is lost and/or gained.

We will make an experiment now by taking a simple paragraph written in the first person and converting it to the third. If we look at Edgar Allen Poe's tales told from the first person point of view, it is impossible to imagine them having the same power narrated from the omniscient point of view. A story like "The Tell-Tale Heart" depends for its power upon the subjectivity of the narrator, a murderous madman whose paranoia and fancy are the essence of the tale. It begins thus:

> True!—nervous—very, very dreadfully nervous I had been and am; but why will you say that I am mad? The disease had sharpened my senses—not destroyed—not dulled them.
> Above all was the sense of hearing acute. I heard all things in heaven and in the earth. I heard many things in hell. How, then, am I mad? Hearken! and observe how healthily—how calmly I can tell you the whole story.
> It is impossible to say how first the idea entered my brain; but once conceived, it haunted me day and night. Object there was none. Passion there was none. I loved the old man. He had never wronged me. He had never given me insult. For his gold I had no desire. I think it was his eye! yes, it was this! One of his eyes resembled that of a vulture—a pale blue eye, with a film over it. Whenever it

fell upon me, my blood ran cold; and so by degrees—very gradually—I made up my mind to take the life of the old man, and thus rid myself of the eye for ever.

We could keep this story in the first person but have it narrated by someone to whom the madman has told his tale. In this case, all that need be changed is the first paragraph, the rest can be left as Poe had it, in the madman's own words. Let's call him Steiner.

True! Steiner had been very dreadfully nervous. But he denied he was mad; he simply claimed that he was and always had been nervous. The disease, he said, had sharpened his senses—not destroyed or dulled them. Above all, he said, was his sense of hearing acute. He claimed to hear all things in heaven and on earth. He heard, so he said, many things in hell. How, then, he asked, could he be mad? He asked us to observe how healthily, how calmly, he told us his story.
"It is impossible," he began, "to say how first the idea entered my brain . . ."

In the process of this modest change, the madman becomes an object, something we observe curiously. Immediacy is lost; the action is distanced. When applied to the theater by writers like Bertolt Brecht, it is called an "alienating device." When Joseph Conrad tells a tale in this fashion, the narrator who begins the story, occasionally interrupts it. The Stage Manager in Thornton Wilder's play, *Our Town*, does the same.

Far more radical alterations in tone and meaning occur when we transfer the narrative into the third person. But third person narratives can differ substantially; varieties emerge depending upon whether or not the omniscient narrator makes judgments on the characters and whether or not the tone is ironic.

Some writers, like Tolstoy, use a narrative voice which sees into the motivations of all characters. Dickens usually follows the same pattern, except for an occasional pretense of ignorance, when the omniscient narrator momentarily disappears. The following excerpt from Martin Chuzzlewit in which the narrator expresses a bit of doubt, is typical.

> With such stimulants to merriment did he beguile the time, and do the honours of the table; while Mr. Pinch, perhaps to assure himself that what he saw and heard was holiday reality, and not a charming dream, ate of everything, and in particular disposed of the slim sandwiches to a surprising extent.

The narrator's "perhaps" is something we would be more likely to encounter in a first-person narrative. (Although there are some first-person narrators, like Mrs. Dean in Wuthering Heights, who are apparently omniscient.)

Another interesting and effective alternative to the choice of first or third person, is Melville's decision in *Moby Dick* to alternate between the two. The novel begins with a first-person narrative by Ishmael that alternates with essay-like accounts on whales and whaling. Soon Melville is writing a third kind of chapter, a narrative in which Ishmael is neither narrator nor participant, with conversations, asides, and whispers to which he could not have been party. Still, with the great language, the imposing scenes and characters, and the self-confidence with which all is told, the shifts are fairly unobtrusive.

Exercise
Take a story you have written and change the person of the narration. Does it work better in first or third person?

EXAGGERATION

Exaggeration is used by many excellent writers to create a reality that has the strength of dreams. It is an element that I stress in workshops, and I always make the point about the strength of exaggeration by having the group read one of Jean Shepherd's stories. Shepherd is a master of comic exaggeration, and the story I usually choose is "Harry Gertz and the Forty-Seven Crappies."

The big joke that runs throughout the story is the pollution in northern Indiana lakes, where blue collar workers, such as the narrator's father and Harry Gertz, like to fish. Pick a passage at random from this story and you almost can be assured that it will contain some joke about the lakes. In one passage, Gertz and the narrator's father are fishing in a lake composed of "roughly ten per cent waste glop spewed out by Shell, Sinclair, Pillips, and the Grasselli Chemical Corporat5ion," plus decomposed snakes, toads and fish. Furthermore:

> It is impossible to sink in this water. The specific gravity and surface tension make the Great Salt Lake seem dangerous for swimming. . . You just bounce a little and float there. You literally have to hit your head on the surface of these lakes to get under a few inches.

Stephen Crane's *Maggie* is another fruitful source for the study of effective exaggeration. In creating the novella's atmosphere of poverty and brutality, Crane exaggerates the elements of his portrait. Consider this opening to the second section of *Maggie*.

> Eventually they entered a dark region where, from a careening building, a dozen gruesome doorways gave up loads of babies to the street and the gutter. A wind of early autumn raised yellow dust from cobbles and swirled it against a hundred windows. Long streamers of garments fluttered from fire escapes. In all unhandy places there were buckets, brooms, rags, and bottles. In the street infants played or fought with other infants or sat stupidly in the way of vehicles. Formidable women, with uncombed hair and disordered dress, gossiped while leaning on railings, or screamed in frantic quarrels. Withered persons, in curious postures of submission to something, sat smoking pipes in obscure corners. A thousand odors of cooking food came forth to the street. The building quivered and creaked from the weight of humanity stamping about in its bowels.

One thing you notice: Crane is not afraid of adjectives and adverbs. A building 'careens,' doorways are 'gruesome,' women are 'formidable,' hair is 'uncombed,' dress is 'disordered,' persons are 'withered' and so on.

It is a visual story. Notice first what Crane does with color, and with light and dark, and how these contribute to the mood. The characters, whoever they are, enter "a dark region." There is "yellow dust. "Over the color and the chiaroscuro effect, Crane layers enormous activity. This dark region swirls with it. Babies, adults, dust, and garments are in motion. Buckets, brooms, and mops are stashed in corners. Even the uncombed hair and disordered dress of the formidable women, the images of withered persons with twisted bodies and smoke curling from their pipes, all suggest motion.

Exercise
1. *Take a story you have written and heighten the tone and mood by exaggerating passages.*
2. *Take a story in public domain and transform it through exaggeration.*

VERB CHOICE

Your choice of verbs greatly affects the tone of your work. They can make it dull or bring it to life. Remember two things about verbs: 1) use the active rather than the passive voice, and 2) search for the appropriate verb to describe the action.

The active voice has the subject acting or doing, e.g. "Jones hit the nail with the hammer," "Margaret gave birth to a baby," and "Billy ran." In the passive voice the subject is acted upon, e.g. "The nail was hit by Jones," "Billy was struck by a car," and "The baby was born." The active voice makes the stronger impression. It is muscular. A work dominated by the passive voice is limp.

The last excerpt from Maggie makes the second point about verbs as well as it can be made. The importance of searching for a verb appropriate to an action cannot be overstressed. Consider someone walking across the street. The person may "strut," "amble," "lope," "truck," "shuffle," "limp," "trot," "step," "plod," "stride," "trudge," and so on. When you have pictured how the person moves, pick your verb. Since the function of writing is to communicate, the more precise we are, the better the writing.

Exercise
Take one of your stories, essays, or poems and see where you have used the passive voice. Substitute the active voice in every instance. Does it strengthen the writing, or does it subvert your meaning?

Look at the same work and see where you can substitute stronger words for those you have.

CHAPTER FIVE
CONVERSATION & DIALOGUE

Many of my students have felt uncomfortable writing dialogue, and it shows by the fact that most of their writing contains very little of it. Occasionally a character will say something, and once in a great while another character will answer, but rarely is there dialogue.

Recently I have been insisting on dialogue as a way of increasing reader interest. Creating good dialogue, having characters speak for themselves, is a way of revealing character. It is generally superior to revelation through narrative, in which the author *tells* us about the characters. We will look at exceptions later. For now let's examine a saying theater people have: Show, don't tell.

To show an activity is to display it. In theater it means presenting the activity on stage. If a competent contemporary playwright has to choose between presenting an activity or having a character describe it, he will choose to present it. Carried over to stories, a writer generally makes a stronger choice by giving us dialogue rather than describing what was said.

Conversation is speech exchanged between people; dialogue is recorded conversation, real or imaginary. Successful dialogue is shaped, and later we will see how some writers have done it. The problem remains: how does one learn to write believable dialogue? The best way is to listen to how people speak. By listening we develop an ear for the rhythms of everyday speech, including repetition, and for the relation between speech and character.

One writer, Lena Leet, has spent almost five days a week, about an hour a day, at a small town café in the rural Midwest, where she enjoys listening to conversations. To understand the following bit of eavesdropping, which she put into play format, you must know that rural America still has lots of active church groups which are the social centers of their communities. As the small town populations in the rural Midwest are now weighted heavily in favor of the elderly, funerals mark the calendars like saints' days. In the Midwest, each church has a committee which makes a meal, usually sandwiches, salads, and desserts, to which everyone at the funeral is invited once the burial is over. These lunches are made by the ladies. Leet says the following conversation was probably between two women who served on their church's food committee.

Two elderly, slender and curly-haired ladies come into the local cafe and sit in a booth.

First Lady: Well, I can't believe they asked the ladies in their eighties to make salads. It should be done by those in their sixties and fifties.

The waitress comes up.

First Lady: Do you have any specials left?
Waitress: They're all gone.
First Lady: They're all gone?
Waitress: It's after 2 o'clock.
Second Lady: We just got out of choir practice. I didn't realize it was so late.

The ladies look at the menu.

First Lady: Well, how about a double bacon cheeseburger? They're awful good. Double bacon cheeseburger.

The second lady looks through the menu. She mumbles.

First Lady: They also have baskets. They have a hamburger basket, a cheeseburger basket, a shrimp

basket, and that's with french fries. The hamburger basket is 3.59 and the shrimp basket is 4.50. That all comes with french fries.
Second Lady: I don't think I want fries.
First Lady: Well then, how about the double bacon cheese burger?

The waitress returns.

First Lady: We're going to have a double bacon cheeseburger. Wait, a double bacon cheeseburger.
Second Lady: Yes, a double bacon cheeseburger. Please bring a knife, we're going to cut it in half.

This brief conversation gives a nice sample of Midwest character. Small town elderly Midwesterners are tight with their money, as are these ladies who make a point of knowing the price of the baskets. Further, as you read the exchange you noticed that the first lady is in control of the relationship, and more or less pressures the second into ordering a double bacon cheeseburger. By the end of the scene it is obvious that before they ordered, the ladies had decided they would share a sandwich. These three observations are excellent keys to establishing the ladies' characters and relationship. You can use such an exchange as the basis of a story.

The next piece of eavesdropping includes a few gestures that help give a picture of the central character, a retired high school teacher who has decided to run for the Iowa state senate. I transcribed the conversation between him, his wife, and other locals while they were having breakfast at another local cafe. We'll call him Sam. Sam's candidacy for the fall election has just been announced in the local paper. To understand this piece you must know that the Iowa caucus is essentially a discussion among members of a political party to determine what issues they want included in their party's national platform.

Sam and his wife sit at one table, friends at a table next to them. Sam is smoking his pipe and looking wise.

Neighbor: Have you been to the state caucus?
Sam: Oh, sure. I was there with [inaudible].
Neighbor: [impressed] Oh yeah?
Sam: Yup.
Neighbor: I'll bet you hear a lot of people shootin' off their mouths.
Sam: Oh, yeah.
Neighbors: All kinds a ideas.
Sam: Extremists.

For the duration of the conversation Sam sits back in his chair, one hand holding his pipe, looking wise.

The truth that this bit of eavesdropping reveals is the fear that rural Iowans have of rocking the boat. Most refuse to stand out, to be different, to speak their minds. That is why Sam's friend used the phrase "shootin' off their mouths" to characterize those who spoke passionately on behalf of an issue. And that is why Sam snapped, "Extremists." He was certifying himself as a middle-of-the-roader who would never make waves. This exchange, like the preceding one, could be used as the basis for a story.

Exercise
1. *Sit with a group of friends or acquaintances and listen to their conversation. Do not talk unless spoken to. Try to memorize what is said and to remember what gestures accompanied the words. Any effort to record what is said or done will be counter-productive. Simply watch and listen. Make a habit of this. Think of yourself as a tape recorder or a camera, as some writers have done. The more you concentrate on listening to conversations the more you will remember them. After each listening session, write down as much of the speech and gestures as you can. You will notice, after recording half a dozen conversations, that you are retaining so much detail that you do not have time to record all of your impressions.*

2. *Take a notebook and visit public places and find conversations in progress. Find a cover for your activity, such as pretending to take notes from a book. Write as fast as you can, in a shorthand of your devising. "Shd" could stand for "should," "wd" for "would," "w/" for "with," and so on. The more you practice transcribing conversations, the easier it becomes. As soon as you can, flesh out the conversation, filling in whatever gaps you can recall. In those places where the missing words are not obvious, make a guess based on the context. You will use these conversations later to construct stories.*

DIALOGUE THAT DOESN'T WORK

Dialogue is conversation that is shaped for literature, whatever the genre. The art of creating believable dialogue is the same for all forms, whether play, novel, story, or essay. But before looking at principles that inhere in good dialogue or effective scenes, we will look at what to avoid. We begin with a scene from an early draft of a memoir written by Rod Haynes, an aspiring California writer with whom I worked through the mail. Rod is looking back at his boyhood.

It was always understood Dad's kids were entirely on his private turf when we entered his art studio, located on the first floor, in a small back corner room of the house closest to Wilbur Road. Dad's attention was riveted on the canvas, as we competed with his art for his input and guidance when we entered his studio.
    I talked to my father about school, friends, sports, and anything else as he twirled and mixed his paints on the palate, squinting at the canvas as he spoke to me: "Well, what did you do today, Rod?"
    "Well, Darrell came over and we went down to Butterfly Pond to go fishing for blue gills," I told him. Blue gills were small fish which were good for little else than hauling out of the water and immediately returning to the pond.
    "Any luck?" he asked, as he mixed a bright yellow acrylic with a Sienna Brown mound which had hardened on

the glass palate and which Dad had softened up by working with warm water. His attention was riveted on the resulting mixture of paint, a pleasant autumnal light brown color which he proceeded to fill his paint brush with.

"Darrell caught two fish, but not me. I never have any luck," I complained. Both of us watched as he squinted at one small part of the canvas, which he filled with his newly mixed paint.

"Uh-huh. Stand over here, Rod, no, over here, away from the light so I can see the canvas. That's good."

"Dad, what does this painting mean?" I asked him, changing the subject.

"Well, tell me what you think it means," he replied with a laugh.

"I don't know, 'cause I can't understand it," I said.

Libby yelled from the dining room: "DAD, JEN, ROD, SETH, COME AND EAT NOW!!! The food is getting cold. Mom says 'NOW.'"

Dad said, "C'mon. We better go wash-up before your mother gets mad." He tossed his paint brush in the paint-spattered coffee can half full of muddy water and paint brushes.

"Okay, Dad," I agreed. Our conversation ended.

Through this incident Haynes intended to illustrate the father's absorption in his art. The scene has great potential, but in this version the writer has not taken advantage of it. As it stands, it has no dramatic movement, which means the characters feel nothing in the course of it. Here is how the dialogue looks by itself.

"Well, what did you do today, Rod?"

"Well, Darrell came over and we went down to Butterfly Pond to go fishing for blue gills."

"Any luck?"

"Darrell caught two fish, but not me. I never have any luck."

"Uh-huh. Stand over here, Rod, no over here,

away from the light so I can see the canvas. That's good."
"Dad, what does this painting mean?"
"Well, tell me what you think it means."
"I don't know, 'cause I can't understand it."
"DAD, JEN, ROD, SETH, COME AND EAT NOW!!! The food is getting cold. Mom says, 'Now.'"
"C'mon. We better go wash-up before your mother gets mad."
"Okay, Dad."

There are three distinct parts, or units, to the conversation. The first concerns fishing.

"Well, what did you do today, Rod?"
"Well, Darrell came over and we went down to Butterfly Pond to go fishing for blue gills."
"Any luck?"
"Darrell caught two fish, but not me. I never have any luck."
"Uh-huh."

The second focuses on the father's art.

"Stand over here, Rod, no over here, away from the light so I can see the canvas. That's good."
"Dad, what does this painting mean?"
"Well, tell me what you think it means."
"I don't know, 'cause I can't understand it."

The third is about going to dinner.

"DAD, JEN, ROD, SETH, COME AND EAT NOW!!! The food is getting cold. Mom says, 'Now.'"
"C'mon We better go wash-up before your mother gets mad."
"Okay, Dad."

The first thing I notice about the dialogue is that there is no emotional or logical connection between the three units. Second, the scene is further weakened by the fact that the boy, who is instigating the conversation by entering the father's private space, makes little attempt to force a conversation. If the boy was this passive in real life, then the writer needs to take us inside the boy's mind, to indicate his desire for connection with his father.

Conflict and Tension

More than a few books on dramatic construction claim that "conflict is the essence of drama," and I have heard numerous directors and actors say the same, even though they have probably directed or acted in scenes which lack conflict. Tension is the essence of drama, but tension is not always conflict. In the previous scene there was neither conflict nor tension. To give that scene power, the writer has to show a discrepancy between what the boy felt and what he said. It is that discrepancy, caused by his fear or inability to verbalize his thoughts, that will create a level of tension.

The fact that the father is absorbed in his painting establishes another level of tension, but his absorption needs to be emphasized. If the boy made an overt attempt to engage the father on an emotional level, the father could evade the move. Rod might have written:

"Dad, can we go fishing someday?"
"Don't you do enough fishing with Darrell? Rod, would you move again. You're in the light."

Tension is now created by the father's avoidance of relationship. I conveyed these thoughts to Mr. Haynes, who wrote the following revision.

It was always understood that Dad's kids were entirely on his exclusive domain when we entered his art studio on the first floor, in a small back corner room of the house. Dad's attention was riveted on the canvas, as we competed with his art for his input and guidance when we entered his studio.

I talked to my father about school, friends, sports, and anything else as he twirled and mixed his paints on the palette, squinting at the canvas as he spoke to me: "Tell me what you did today, Rod," his attention and interest squarely on the painting in front of him. I stood behind Dad, near the large, bright lamp illuminating the open space, which was clamped to the edge of his large drawing table. The lamp could be tilted in any direction, providing optimal lighting as Dad worked his paintings. I was unaware that I was partially blocking the illumination of the canvas Dad was working on.

"Well, Darrell came over and we went down to Butterfly Pond to go fishing for blue gills." Blue gills were small fish which were good for little else than hauling out of the water and immediately returning to the pond.

"Any luck?" he asked, as he mixed a bright yellow acrylic with a Sienna brown mound which had hardened on the glass palette and which Dad had softened up by working with warm water. He worked briskly to produce a pleasant autumnal light brown color with which he proceeded to fill his paint brush.

"Darrell caught two fish, but not me. I never have any luck," I complained, wondering if anything I was saying was registering with him. He squinted at one small part of the canvas, which he proceeded to busily fill with his newly mixed paint. Several minutes passed as he wiped away an excess amount of acrylic with a rag and in a barely audible voice said, "Damn, no, no, no." At that point I felt awkward, like I was disrupting his work. Maybe I should talk to him later.

Recovering his thoughts, he looked over his shoulder at me and, picking up where he had left off several minutes ago, said, "Oh, uh-huh. Stand over here, Rod. No, over here, away from the light so I can see the canvas. That's good."

This wasn't going very well. My ten-year old mind wondered how better to connect with him. What if I talked about something he liked?

"Dad, what does this painting mean?" I asked him.

"Well, tell me what YOU think it means," he replied with a laugh. That seemed to liven the discussion.

"I don't know, because I can't understand it," I said.

Seconds later we were mercifully interrupted when Libby yelled from the dining room: "DAD, JEN, ROD, SETH, COME AND EAT NOW!!! The food is getting cold. Mom says NOW."

Dad said, "C'mon. We better go wash-up before your mother gets anxious." He tossed his brush in the paint-spattered coffee can half full of muddy water and brushes.

"Okay, Dad."

With the addition of a few sentences which give the boy's feelings, Rod gives inner life to the character while creating tension within the scene. Because of it the scene now works, despite only one addition to the dialogue, the father's "Damn, no, no no." This episode is now largely an interior mood piece.

A very different story was created in a three-day workshop in Helena, Arkansas. The author, Nashid Madyun, is former education director for the Delta Cultural Center, an agency of the Arkansas Department of Heritage and the workshop's sponsor. With a wonderful cross section of blacks and whites from varying backgrounds, this workshop yielded enough material to make a strong little book. One of the successes of Nashid's piece lies in its effective integration of dialogue within a story focused on action.

His two young characters, a boy and girl, live in Helena, which lies on the Mississippi River, which accounts for the levee. When the boy suggests they go to his house for paper, it is because he wants to make boats with it. This fact helps explain the difference between the two characters.

The next day I was walking back from Glorioso's store on Walker's levee, and here comes Latonya Hill on her bike almost jumping the levee.

"Get on," she demanded. Latonya was nine years old, and could do anything a boy could do, but could not beat me running. This fact of life brought me more attention from Tonya than my life deserved. She had one of those dirt bikes with the "mag rims." The rims, originally pink, had white streaks painted on them, which hid any "girly" appearances.

"You want to go to the dam?" I asked.

"Wherever," she said confidently. She was not afraid of anything.

"Let's go to my house first so I can get some paper," I suggested, not knowing that Tonya had other plans.

"You gettin' on?" she asked, staring directly at me, then leaning forward on her handle bars.

"Yeah." I didn't really want to get on. I could walk. But for some reason I could never say no to Tonya. Plus, she was older.

We made it to the dam, but not before a small test of will on Tonya's part. A strong kid could pull Walker's levee with someone on the back of the bike with no problem. Tonya made me get off. She said she wanted me to see how fast she could pull it, and that it did not count if I was on the back.

"A new record," she screamed, though I had nothing to compare it to.

At the dam Tonya and I stood staring at the water. "Here is some paper," I offered. Tonya had little interest in my paper games.

"Hold up, let's try something first." Tonya looked around the floodgate until she found some rocks. I got the biggest bunch. "Can you hit the top of the stairs?" Tonya reminded me that she did it all the time. The floodgate had a small tower that had iron stairs on the west side. We threw about three loads of rocks each. I probably hit the stairs ten times, but I only hit the top once. Tonya hit the top—three glorious times.

"Let's climb the stairs," Tonya demanded. I was afraid of heights. Once we reached the top I realized that Tonya was even more afraid. I had overcome my fear and was ready to go back down. Tonya, with tears in her eyes, said, "I really like it up here." We had to sit and like it up there for nearly two hours. The sun had stopped beating and the distance down was not as far anymore. We both made it to the bottom and looked at each other. I smiled, close to laughter.

"Come on," yelled Tonya. She was ready to go home. I got on the back of the bike and Tonya pedaled away. She stopped all of a sudden at the top of Walker's levee, near Glorioso's store. "Get off," Tonya demanded.

As I got off, Tonya turned to me and said, "You better not tell no one." She hit me on the lip and flew off on her bike down the north side of Walker's levee toward Profitt Drive where she lived.

There is tension here between the characters, and it is revealed through both the dialogue and the boy's thoughts. Dialogue and thoughts together create and reveal character and are matched with the physical activity.

The girl's character is established quickly: "'Get on,' she demanded." It doesn't take long for us to understand that the boy is a bit awed and slightly cowed by her. She "could do anything a boy could do, but could not beat me running. This fact of life brought me more attention from Tonya than my life deserved." Here is the first unit of the story.

"You want to go to the dam?" I asked.

"Wherever," she said confidently.

"Let's go to my house first so I can get some paper," I suggested.

"You gettin' on?" she asked, staring directly at me, then leaning forward on her handle bars.

"Yeah." I didn't really want to get on. I could walk. But for some reason I could never say no to Tonya. Plus, she was older.

The boy initiates the action by asking if Tonya wants to go to the dam; she accepts. He wants to go home to get paper, but she will have none of it. She immediately takes command of the scene. "You gettin' on?" Her words and action—staring and leaning forward—mark the point of maximum tension for the unit. When the boy answers, "Yes," the tension subsides. A unit is defined by the rise and fall of tension. In an effectively written scene, they are clearly discernible. A good scene in a play or story will have tension flowing through it, at times invisible, at times intense. No scene of direct conflict can carry on effectively if the characters yell continuously at each other. No scene with a constant minimum of tension can succeed in maintaining interest. A good writer knows better than to keep the tension at a constant level. That does not mean that the writers are consciously thinking about tension. Nashid did not, but he had read enough good literature and heard enough good story tellers to intuitively be able to craft an effective work. A unit may sometimes be marked by a change of subject in discussion or by a tactic in debate. For now it is enough for you to be aware that tension must rise and fall.

The next unit in the present story are the two paragraphs describing the girl's ride to the top of the dam, first forcing the boy off the bike, then racing up the hill and screaming that she has set a new record. Here the conflict between the two is first direct, when she orders him off the bike, then indirect as she races up the hill and claims a record. The point of maximum tension comes when she screams, "A new record." The clause that follows—"though I had nothing to compare it with"—gives a release of tension and preparation for the next unit. Its effectiveness can be judged by the fact that if you end that sentence after "she screamed," we would not have a nice underlining to her boastfulness, we would not have a transition to the next unit, and we would not have a lessening of tension.

Exercise
1. *Create two characters with a relationship like the father and son: perhaps a mother and a daughter, older and younger siblings, a husband and wife, any relationship in which one hopes for nurturing or caring. Find an activity for the older person and have the younger one initiate the conversation. He or she has a*

need. What is it? Do not express the need in words. Instead, let us discover it in the tension between the spoken words and unspoken thoughts and feelings you describe.
2. Identify the remaining units in Nashid's story, and identify the point of maximum tension.

MOVE AND RESISTANCE

In *Shakespeare's Game*, playwright William Gibson gives an excellent account of Shakespeare's dramaturgy. He resolves the dynamic elements of a scene into Move and Object. In Gibson's analysis, the Move initiates the action. The characters) upon which it acts is the Object. The Move may try to persuade the Object to take a certain point of view, to take a certain action, to desist from taking action, and so on. In a surprisingly similar analysis, *The Dynamics of Drama* by Bernard Beckerman, the Object is called the Resistance. "Resistance" is the word I use, because it highlights the tension that exists within effective scenes.

Here is a scene from Stephen Crane's novella, *Maggie*, which has a clearly defined Move and Resistance.

> A forlorn woman went along a lighted avenue. The street was filled with people desperately bound on missions. An endless crowd darted at the elevated train station stairs, and the horsecars were thronged with owners of bundles.
> The pace of the forlorn woman was slow. She was apparently searching for someone. She loitered near the doors of saloons and watched men emerge from them. She furtively scanned the faces in the rushing stream of pedestrians. Hurrying men, bent on catching some boat or train, jostled her elbows, failing to notice her, their thoughts fixed on distant dinners.
> The forlorn woman had a peculiar face. Her smile was no smile. But when in repose, her features had a shadowy look that was like a sardonic grin, as if someone had sketched with cruel forefinger indelible lines about her mouth.
> Jimmie came strolling up the avenue. The woman

encountered him with an aggrieved air. "Oh, Jimmie, I've been lookin' all over for yehs—" she began.

Jimmie made an impatient gesture and quickened his pace. "Ah, don't bodder me!" he said, with the savageness of a man whose life is pestered.

The woman followed him along the sidewalk in somewhat the manner of a suppliant. "But, Jimmie," she said, "yehs told me yehs—"

Jimmie turned upon her fiercely as if resolved to make a last stand for comfort and peace. "Say, Hattie, don' foller me from one end of deh city teh deh odder. Let up, will yehs! Give me a minute's res', can't yehs? Yehs makes me tired, allus taggin' me. See? Go chase yerself."

The woman stepped closer and laid her fingers on his arm. "But, look a' here—"

Jimmie snarled. "Oh, go teh blazes!" He darted into the front door of a convenient saloon and a moment later came out into the shadows that surrounded the side door. On the brilliantly lighted avenue, he perceived the forlorn woman dodging about like a scout. Jimmie laughed with an air of relief and went away.

In this scene the ruined woman, Hattie, is the Move and Jimmie is the Object. But Hattie is at the end of her tether and without force. Whenever she attempts to speak, Jimmie cuts her off. She has not the power to complete her sentences or overcome his resistance. In the end, he dismisses her with a snarl and an "Oh, go te blazes!" and walks off, only to laugh at her pathetic attempts to find him outside the saloon.

The dialogue by itself is short and brutal.

"Oh, Jimmie, I've been lookin' all oveh for yehs—"
"Ah, don't bodder me!"
"But, Jimmie, yehs told me yehs—"
"Say, Hattie, don't foller me from one end of deh city teh deh odder. Let up, will yehs! Give me a minute's res', can't yehs? Yehs makes me tired, allus taggin' me. See? Ain' yehs

got no sense? Do yehs want people teh get on me? Go chase yehself."

"But, look a' here—"

"Oh, go teh blazes!"

Jimmie's first response to Hattie is "Ah, don't bodder me!" But when that fails to run her off, he resorts to reasoning with her. He says she is tiring him by following him from one end of the city to the other; furthermore, if she doesn't let up, people are likely to bother him because he has ruined her. Doesn't she have any concern for him? When she pleads once again, he tells her to go to blazes and runs off.

If Jimmie had not given her this defense, but had uttered another variation of "Don't bodder me!" the exchange would have been far less dramatic. By telling Hattie that she is exhausting him and about to get him in trouble, we learn about Jimmie. When character is revealed through action, we have drama.

Jimmie is the protege of another Bowery tough and man of the world, Pete, who has taken a fancy to Jimmie's sister Maggie. After luring her from her home to live with him, he meets an old flame and abandons Maggie. Maggie, fearful, returns home. The previous scene is followed by this:

When he returned home, he found his mother clamoring. Maggie had returned. She stood shivering beneath the torrent of her mother's wrath.

"Well, I'm damned!" said Jimmie in greeting.

His mother, tottering about the room, pointed a quivering forefinger. "Look ut her, Jimmie, look ut her. Dere's yer sister, boy. Dere's yer sister. Look ut her! Look ut her!" She screamed at Maggie with scoffing laughter.

The girl stood in the middle of the room. She edged about as if unable to find a place on the floor to put her feet.

"Ha ha, ha!" bellowed the mother. "Dere she stands! Ain't she purty? Look ut her! Ain't she purty? Look ut her! Ain' she sweet, deh beast? Look ut her! Ha, ha! Look ut her!" She lurched forward and put her red and seamed hands upon her daughter's face. She bent down and peered keenly up into the eyes of the girl. "Oh, she's jes de same as she ever was, ain't she? She's her mudder's purty darlin' yit, ain' she? Look ut her, Jimmie. Come here and look ut her."

The loud, tremendous railing of the mother brought the denizens of the Rum Alley tenement to their doors. Women came in the hallways. Children scurried to and fro.

"What's up? Dat Johnson party on anudder tear?"

"Naw. Young Mag's come home!"

"Git out!"

Through the open doors, curious eyes stared in at Maggie. Children ventured into the room and ogled her as if they formed the front row at a theatre. Women, without, bent toward each other and whispered, nodding their heads with airs of profound philosophy.

. . . . .

Maggie's mother paced to and fro, addressing the doorful of eyes, expounding like a glib showman. Her voice rang through the building. "Dare she stands," she cried, wheeling suddenly and pointing with dramatic finger. "Dere she stands! Look ut her! Ain' she a dandy? An' she was so good as to come home teh her mudder, she was! Ain' she a beaut'? Ain't she a dandy?"

The jeering cries ended in another burst of shrill laughter.

The girl seemed to awaken. "Jimmie—"

He drew hastily back from her. "Well, now, yer a t'ing, ain' yeh?" he said, his lips curing in scorn. Radiant virtue sat upon his brow, and his repelling hands expressed horror of contamination.

Maggie turned and went.

. . . .

As the girl passed down through the hall, she went before open doors framing more eyes strangely microscopic . . . On the second floor she met the gnarled old woman who possessed the music box.

"So," she cried, "'ere yehs are back again, are yehs? An' dey've kicked yehs out? Well, come in an' stay wid me t'night. I ain' got no moral standin'."

From above came an unceasing babble of tongues, over all of which rang the mother's derisive laughter.

This scene mirrors the previous one. Maggie, like Hattie, has come to the people she thinks might protect her and, like Hattie, is rejected. Jimmie, who has ruined Hattie, finds nothing in himself to condemn. He is virtuous and therefore must reject his own sister. In fact, everyone in the Rum Alley tenement, down to the old woman, reject and humiliate her.

Like Hattie in her scene with Jimmie, Maggie is the Move in her scene. Since, by the conventions of nineteenth-century society, a woman in Maggie's position is a social pariah and a family disgrace, her Move has little force. She stands mute in the presence of her tormentors.

Exercise

Write a scene with a clearly defined Move and Resistance. You may write it entirely in dialogue form with a few stage directions, or you may write it in narrative form. Make the Move weak, like Maggie and Hattie, and create a strong, perhaps brutal Resistance, like Jimmie and his mother. First determine the protagonist, who is your Move. Perhaps it is based on someone you have observed. He or she has gotten into some kind of trouble. What is it? The Resistance is a family member or friend to whom they appeal for help. Their plea is rejected.

Envision the protagonist. What does he or she look like? How has their problem affected their posture or gestures. What is their posture? Do they have a gesture which they repeat over and over?

Describe the setting. Does it enhance the mood of the protagonist or is it at variance with it?

The Resistance enters. Is it a man or woman? How do they move? Quickly? Deliberately? Nonchalantly?

The Move speaks first. What does he or she say? What reply, if any, does the Resistance make?

Begin writing.

ACCENT AND DIALECT

A lot of great American realistic writing of the nineteenth and twentieth centuries imitated both regional accents and dialects. By accent I mean a pattern of pronunciation. Someone with an accent may or may not speak standard English. Born and bred Bostonians have a pronounced accent, but plenty of them speak grammatically standard English. By definition the person speaking dialect does not speak standard English, but a variant.

Writing a story in dialect from the narrator's point of view is simply an extension of imitating another person's speech. Young people are natural mimics; as we get older, we get more self-conscious and have to relearn the skill. I am suggesting that you try it now. If you have grown up listening to one dialect all your life begin by imitating that.

A number of successful writers of accent and dialect, including Damon Runyon, have done that. Runyon, a famous New York sports writer of the 1930s and 40s, listened to a lot of bookies and underworld types on Broadway. Their patois became the basis for a narrative voice that he used in his numerous short stories about Broadway habitués. The voice is that of a low status character (a gangster or bookie, for example) trying to play a high status character (a college professor or lawyer). Runyon conveys the character of the narrator by having him speak with a certain stiffness, which comes in part from not using contractions. We infer from his awkward attempts at grammatical propriety that the narrator thinks that high status characters avoid contractions. Thus he creates his absurd speech. It reminds us of the Three Stooges or Laurel and Hardy at a black tie dinner, trying to pass themselves off as society types. Because they don't know the rules and haven't observed the society types closely, they have ridiculous ideas of how society types talk and behave.

A number of characters reappear throughout Runyon's stories, and were the basis for the Broadway musical, *Guys and Dolls*. This excerpt is from a Runyon story called "Romance in the Roaring Forties."

> Only a rank sucker will think of taking two peeks at
> Dave the Dude's doll, because while Dave may stand for

the first peak, figuring it is a mistake, it is a sure thing he will get sored up at the second peak, and Dave the Dude is certainly not a man to have sored up at you.

If you have seen 1940s Hollywood comedies with the comic gangster as a secondary character, you will hear his stereotyped voice in this narrator.

A more complicated level of dialect writing is represented in the work of Ring Lardner, another New York newspaper man, who grew up in Indiana and spent his early working years in Chicago. Lardner was also a short story writer, some of whose best know stories are "Haircut," "Gullible's Travels," and "Three Without, Doubled." Lardner's work in dialect is confined to a variety of Midwestern speech, specifically to working class speech. "Gullible's Travels" begins in this way:

I promised the Wife that if anybody ast me what kind of a time did I have at Palm Beach I'd say I had a swell time. And if they ast me who did we meet I'd tell 'em everybody that was worth meetin'. And if they ast me didn't the trip cost a lot I'd say Yes; but it was worth the money. I promised her I wouldn't spill none o' the real details. But if you can't break a promise you made to your own wife what kind of a promise can you break? Answer me that, Edgar.

I'm not one o' these kind o' people that'd keep a joke to themself just because the joke was on them. But they're plenty of our friends that I wouldn't have 'em hear about it for the world. I wouldn't tell you, only I know you're not the village gossip and won't crack it to anybody. Not even to your own missus, see? I don't trust no women.

It was along last January when I and the Wife was both hit by the society bacillus. I think it was at the opera. You remember me tellin' you about us and that Hatches goin' to *Carmen* and then me takin' my Missus and her sister, Bess, and four of one suit named Bishop to see *The Three Kings*? Well, I'll own up that I enjoyed wearin' the soup and fish and minglin' among the high polloi and pretendin' we really

was somebody. And I know my wife enjoyed it, too, though they was nothin' said between us at the time."
The next stage was where our friends wasn't good enough for us no more."

That's the setup. The narrator and his wife are probably middle to low status characters. From the last line we know that they want to be high status, and much of the comedy of this story derives from seeing these two fish out of water trying to act as though they belong to high society.

A bit later the Wife gets an idea about taking a vacation. She starts talking to him about their savings, and he tells her:

"It'd be a mistake to let loose now," I says.
"All right," she says. "Hold on, and I hope you lose every cent. You never did care nothin' for me."
Then we done a little spoonin' and then I ast her what was the big idear.
"We ain't swelled on ourself," she says, "but I know and you know that the friends we been associatin' with ain't in our class. They don't know how to dress and they can't talk about nothin' but their goldfish and their meat bills. They don't try to get nowheres, but all they do is play rummy and take in the Majestic. I and you like nice people and good music and things that's worthw'ile. It's a crime for us to be wastin' our time with riff and raff that'd run round barefooted if it wasn't for the police."

A few writers have a truly gifted ear and are able not only to record the rhythms and patterns of words in a dialect, but are able to record the sounds phonetically. Peter Finley Dunne, a Chicago journalist, was a master of dialect writing. In the late nineteenth century, Dunne began writing sketches in Irish dialect spoken by Dunne's character, Mr. Dooley. Mr. Dooley's pronouncements on social and political issues were enormously popular and President Theodore Roosevelt was among Dunne's regular readers. Here is the opening of a sketch with Dooley addressing his interlocutor,

Mr. Hennessey.

> "I wondher," said Mr. Dooley, "what me Dutch frind Oom Paul'll think whin he hears that Willum Waldorf Asthor has given four thousan' pounds or twinty thousan' iv our money as a conthribution to th' British governmint?"
> "Who's Willum Waldorf Asthor?" Mr. Hennessy asked. "I niver heerd iv him."
> "Ye wudden't," said Mr. Dooley. "He don't thravel in ye'er set. Willum Waldorf Asthor is a gintleman that wanst committed th' sin iv bein' bor-rn in this counthry. Ye know what orig-inal sin is, Hinnissy. Ye was bor-rn with wan an' I was bor-rn with wan an' ivrybody was bor-rn with wan. 'Twas took out iv me be Father Tuomy with holy wather first an' be me father aftherward with a sthrap. But I niver cud find out what it was.

Some of the best examples of dialect writing are found in the Uncle Remus stories of Joel Chandler Harris, who grew up in the South and listened carefully to black speech. Harris's stories are told by Uncle Remus to a little white boy, which explains the boy's interruption in the story below, "The End of Mr. Bear."

> " . . . One time when Brer Rabbitt wuz gwine lopin' home fum a frolic w'at dey bin havin' up at Miss Meadow's, who should he happin' up wid but ole Brer B'ar. Co'se, atter w'at done pass 'twix um dey wa'n't no good feelin's 'tween Brer Rabbitt en ole Brer B'ar, but Brer Rabbitt, he wanter save his manners, en so he holler out:
> "Heyo, Brer B'ar! how you come on? I ain't seed you in a coon's age. How all down at yo' house? How Miss Brune en Miss Brindle?"
> "Who was that, Uncle Remus?" the little boy interrupted.
> "Miss Brune en Miss Brindle? Miss Brune wuz Brer B'ar's ole 'oman, en Miss Brindle wuz his gal. Dat w'at dey call um in dem days. So den Brer Rabbit, he ax him howdy, he did, en Brer B'ar, he 'spon' dat he wuz mighty

po'ly, en dey amble 'long, dey did, sorter familious like, but Brer Rabbit, he keep one eye on Brer B'ar, he study how he gwine nab Brer Rabbit. 'Las' Brer Rabbit, he up'n say, sezee:

" 'Brer B'ar, I speck I got some bizness cut out fer you,' sezee.

" 'What dat, Brer Rabbit?' sez Brer B'ar, sezee.

" 'Wiles I wuz cleanin' 'cross wunner deze yer old time bee-trees. Hit start holler at de bottom, en stay holler plum der de top, en de honey's des naturally oozin' out, en ef you'll drap yo 'gagements en go 'longer me,' sez Brer Rabbit, sezee, 'you'll git a bait dat'll las' you en yo' fambly twel de middle er nex' mont',' sezee.

"Brer B'ar say he much oblije en he b'leeve he'll go 'long, en wid dat dey put out fer Brer Rabbit's new-groun', w'ich twa'b't so mighty fur. Leas'ways, dey got dar atter w'ile. Ole Brer B'ar, he 'low dat he kin smell de honey. Brer Rabbit, he 'low dat he kin see de honey-koam. Brer B'ar, he 'low dat he can hear de bees a zoomin'. Dey stan' 'roun' en talk biggity, dey did, twel bimeby Brer Rabbit, he up'n say, sezee:

"You do de clim-'in', Brer B'ar, en I'll do de rushin' 'roun'; you clime up ter de hole, en I'll take dis yer pine pole en shove de honey up whar you kin git git 'er', sezee.

"Ole Brer B'ar, he spit on his han's en skint up de tree, en jam his head in de hole, en sho nuff, Brer Rabbit, he grab de pine pole, en de way he stir up dem bees wuz sinful— dat's w'at it wuz. Hit wuz sinful. En de bees dey swamm'd on Brer B'ar's head, twel fo' he could take it out'n de hole hit wuz done swell up biggerr dan dat dinner-pot, en dar he swung, en ole Brer Rabbit, he dance 'roun' en sing:

" 'Tree stan' high, but honey mighty sweet—
Watch dem bees wid stingers on der feet.'

"But dar ole Brer B'ar hung, en ef his head ain't swunk, I speck he hangin' dar yit—dat w'at I speck."

During the Great Depression of the 1930s, Franklin D.

96 THE WRITER WITHIN

Roosevelt's administration created the Works Progress Administration, which employed millions of jobless men and women with blue and white collar public works projects. The blue-collar projects included the creation of dams, public schools and recreational areas, while the white-collar projects employed artists, writers and musicians to create and perform plays, paint public murals, compose music, write books. One of the book projects employed writers to interview 2,000 former slaves and to transcribe their interviews. The complete collection is available for viewing at the Library of Congress. A sample has been collected in the volume, *When I was a Slave: Memoirs from the Slave Narrative Collection*, edited by Norman R. Yetman. Here is a sample of the speech of one ex-slave, John Finnely.

> "Massa use me for huntin' and use me for de gun rest. When him have de long shot I bends over and puts de hands on de knees and Massa puts his gun on my back for to get de good aim. When him kills I runs and fetches and carries de game for him...
>
> "All dat not so bad, but when he shoots de duck in de water and I has to fetch it out, dat give me de worriment. Dat first time he tells me to go in the pond I'se skeert, powerful skeert. I takes off de shirt and pants but there I stands. I steps in the water, den back again, and again. Massa am gettin' mad. He say, 'Swim in dere and get dat suck.' 'Yes,, sir, Massa,' I says, but I won't go in dat water till Massa hit me some licks."

Exercise
1. *Try to identify some of your own speech patterns—words you repeat, your pronunciation, your pauses, and so on. Work in tandem with someone else. Point your patterns out to one another.*
2. *What other devices, besides the avoidance of contractions, does Runyon use to create awkward speech? And what does he use besides stiff speech to convey the narrator's status?*
3. *Take a newspaper editorial and put it in the mouth of a low status*

character. You may chose to imitate Runyon's model, or you may chose a voice with which you are familiar. Have the character pretend to be educated and a person of the world. Exaggerate. Have fun.
4. Take a page from a favorite story with narration and dialogue written in standard English. Rewrite it from the point of view of someone who speaks with an accent or in a dialect, preferably someone from your own locale or region. Spell some of the words phonetically.

CHAPTER SIX
MEMOIR WRITING

In recent years there has been an explosion of memoir writing in this country, most of it by elders. But whether the writer is elderly or not, the work appears to be done in response to our culture's extraordinary rate of social and technological change. It appears that by writing records of their lives, and thereby preserving a record of the past, the authors are attempting to maintain a kind of psychological stability in the ever shifting present.

Memoirs by elders have historical and anthropological value, providing first-hand data for future historians. Even personal stories by young people, if psychologically revealing, provide the same. If you write your story as though you are trying to provide future readers not only entertainment but a knowledge of your times, you will add an extra dimension to your work. It will also help you to cull unimportant material, because by asking, "What would people a hundred years from now care to know?" you will be led to realize which stories have a merely personal interest. The last section in this chapter deals with this and other editing questions.

STARTING THE MEMOIR

When you begin your memoir, write as much as you can without thinking about the book's organization. Arrange your writing later, after you have accumulated a large amount of material.

If you are starting a memoir with a strong desire to write it, discovering what to record will not be difficult. Simply write the stories as they occur to you. Do not try to discriminate between good or bad, important or unimportant. Your goal is to amass as much material as you can, as quickly as you can.

After having written a large number of pieces, most likely you will come to a point when you think you have run out of material or energy. It is only natural for a writer to tire of a project after working intensely on it for several months. If that is the case, simply lay the manuscript aside and work on something else to let the project percolate. If, on the other hand, you are not tired but have run out of ideas, make lists of people, events, and places that were important in your life. Seeing names will remind you of other people, events, and places.

You may think that certain events in your life happened so long ago that you cannot remember them in detail. My experience, and that of the writers with whom I have worked, is that the more you write about your past, the more you will remember. Try to recall conversations, as these usually increase the drama in your scenes. If you cannot recall what was actually said, write what was most likely said. If the scene represents a recurring situation, write the kind of dialogue that typifies it. The dialogue between the father and son by Rod Haynes in the chapter on conversation was not actual, but represented the kind of exchange that did occur.

There are four parts to creating a book of memoirs. The first consists of writing stories and reflections, the second of arranging them chronologically, the third of determining a theme, and the fourth of eliminating irrelevant material and expanding stories that need to be enlarged.

WRITING THE STORIES

I have worked with five writers on book-length memoirs. Three of them decided from the outset to write in the most natural way to compose a memoir, which is to create a collection of relatively short anecdotes that can stand on their own. It is also the most natural method because we remember our lives as a series of short short stories. Since we do not remember them in chronological order, I advise people to begin their memoirs by writing stories as they occur to them, in whatever sequence.

This was the method used by Murray Hudson in writing an account of his twelve years raising cotton in West Tennessee, *Dirt*

& Duty: Or How I Came to Love the Land and Loathe Farming. His stories or observations and essays usually ran between three and eight paragraphs. Typically they were profiles of individuals, records of local ways of doing things, descriptions of places, accounts of events, or nature observations. As you write your recollections and observations, you will find them naturally falling into one or more of these categories. Occasionally categories overlap.

Write vignettes in all categories. By doing so you will produce a fuller picture of the world than you would otherwise.

PROFILE OF INDIVIDUALS

It is easy to begin by writing profiles of people, such as Murray Hudson's sketch of Son Ozmont in chapter three. In the chapter on strategies we looked at the introduction to Jerry Crabb's story about his black nanny. Here it is in its entirety.

> Lovey Johnson was our black mama. She helped raise the four of us with the threatened discipline of a green switch coupled with innumerable helpings of corn bread and navy beans. She was one of an endless stream of surrogate mothers in the segregated South.
>
> To keep four children (three boys and a girl) clothed and fed, my real mother had to go to work at two back-to-back jobs. Because of our oft-disappearing alcoholic father, Lovey was the answer to a prayer, simply a god-send. How else, if not for Lovey, would mother be able to sit at a sewing machine at the Bobbie Brooks garment factory all day and then later enshrine herself within the ticket booth of the Paramount Theater at night? In those Eisenhower days of Davy Crockett coonskin caps, poodle skirts, and hula hoops, women were very much at the lower end of the economic ladder. So much more so if that woman were black.
>
> The black nanny had by the 1950's long been a Southern institution. Even the poorest, most down-on-their-luck white family such as ours could often afford a black maid-cum-babysitter such as Lovey, so very low were the wages that a black worker of that day might expect. How Lovey ever

managed to survive is one of my life's mysteries.

Lovey lived, in my earliest memory of her, in one of a row of shotgun-style houses facing the edge of a concrete city drainage ditch, these shanties placed just behind the white houses that fronted outward on the 800-block of Walnut Street. South Africa would have its apartheid, the Delta these ditch-row dwellings.

Lovey was short and plump, with, over the years, two ever-worsening arthritic hands that finally became two gnarled, hardly usable appendages at the ends of her arms. She used to iron our clothes with crippled hands that could hardly hold onto the iron, for she could barely force her curled fingers to open. Her constant smiles were often tight-lipped ones, partly of pain and partly to hold back dips of Garrett snuff. Her favored woolen socks bought at the local dime store drooped in quiet counterpoint to the usual white blouse that somehow was never stained by any errant snuff.

She was unmarried, childless, but must have had siblings for I believe it was a niece in New Orleans with whom she lived out her last years, battling the arthritis to the end. Lovey was not certain of her own age and had had little or no formal education; my mother, with only an eighth grade education herself, would help Lovey finally receive her social security benefits.

Through all of the various infirmities and indignities her life would bring her, I am left ever with the image of a steady warmth and care, this image broken only with the occasional outburst of anger toward the latest devilment my younger brother, Bill, may have performed. "You so mannish!" she'd tell him before sending him out for a switch for his latest chastisement. Once Bill locked himself in a trunk to hide from Lovey's wrath and then couldn't get out, for the trunk had locked on him. Then my brother had to decide whether it was better to yell for help or to simply suffocate to death.

Lovey was to be a part of our lives for more than thirteen years, preparing biscuits and butter for our after-school treats, giving us nickels to buy Jackson lemon cookies at the corner grocery, smiling good-naturedly on us day after day. It was no wonder then that one of the first acts of my marriage was to take my new wife to Lovey's house to pay our respects. My wife said later that she got the real impression that she was being inspected by "that little woman" to see if "I was good enough for you."

"Yeah," I thought to myself, "mothers are like that."

Exercise
Write a profile of someone who had a big influence on your life. You can do this in one of two ways: either write a paragraph on each important aspect of their character or illustrate their character by describing an event in which the person played a pivotal role.

EVENTS

Descriptions of events will form the backbone of your memoir. Particular happenings will not pose a problem. Describe what you remember, including only as much detail as you need to make your point. A problem arises, however, when you try to describe typical events. For example, you might write: "Whenever Sherry and I upset Mother, she would say, 'You two are a pack of trouble.'" Or: "The first thing Uncle John always did after a fishing trip was to scale and gut the catch." Or: "Sam and Bernice would make a point of visiting us whenever they came to Lake Geneva." Suppose you set up a typical event in such a fashion and then launched into dialogue. How would you treat it? As typical but not actual? Or would you record to the best of your recollection what actually was said on one such day?

One writer created a confusing scene of a recurring event by beginning it with verb forms such as "would arrive," "would go," "would recite," and so on. Then, in order to create drama, she launched into dialogue. But the dialogue did not contain verb forms such as "would say," but "said." This meant that the writer switched from typical to specific. The switch was jarring and disturbing. It did not work.

Here is my paraphrase and condensation of her scene:

> Every evening after Dad came home from work he would head first to the refrigerator where he would grab a beer. He would start talking to Mom, who would be fixing supper. This was the time of day for Mom to give Dad her report on the kids. Every day the form of conversation was about the same.
> "Well," Dad asked, "how were the kids today?"
> "It's been a crazy day," Mom replied. "Janey fell off the jungle gym at school and broke an arm, Johnny acted up in class and was sent to the principal's office, and Ryan was truant."

You need to stick with one verb form or the other. Murray Hudson solved this problem by describing a particular day, and through the title let us know that it was typical. Calling one vignette "A Day in the Life of a Farmer," solved the problem for that piece.

By putting that and other pieces into the present tense, he increased interest. But by putting other stories in the past, he gave two layers of texture to his memoir. Added to the variation of tenses are occasional prose poems and catalogues, which contribute two more textures to the whole. The following story in the past tense is from *Dirt & Duty*.

> *All That Bull*
> Roundup on our farm was chaos. My father had managed to cull out most of the docile cattle, the ones that would actually walk through the chutes and load in a cattle truck for market. By the time I came back the renegades and yearling bulls made the gathering and shipping of cattle a nightmare.
> We had one young Charlois bull who should have been cut a year or so earlier, but here he was rampaging into the barn lot at roundup scaring the socks off the men. They didn't help much by following their north Mississippi version of cattle herding by whacking down eight-foot saplings, stripping the limbs and leaves and wielding these homemade whips behind the antsy herd while yelling, "Whoopee!

Get on there you durn heifer."

I finally decided that I could teach the men a lesson, having in mind my expertise learned on my father-in-law's ranch in Arizona, testing his Brahma herd for brucellosis, where they tore down chutes and gates built for smaller, tamer Herefords. I told them that the young bull had their bluff, and, if they just stood their ground, he would not harm them.

They all three yelled, "Here he comes!" and jumped the corral fence. Around the corner of the barn swung the thousand pounds of cotton-white fury, kicking up puffs of dust in his wake. I stood in the middle of the barn lot, hands folded across my chest. I was convinced that he would stop short of me, and he did, close enough that I could feel the heat of his snorting breath. "See, I told you he was all bluff," I announced proudly. The men stayed quietly on the backside of the five-foot fence.

Then the bull stuck his right hoof out and planted it squarely on the toe of my leather boot. He, hornless, thank God, then proceeded to butt me in the gut while holding me up with the hoof of my boot. Since he knocked the wind out of me, I couldn't make a sound. If I could, it would have drowned in the men's gut-rumbling laughter.

I have run numerous workshops for farmers over the past decade, and others have written good stories about cattle. Dorothy Sandry has been a farm wife for many years, and with her husband, Richard, participated in a farm writing workshop in northeast Iowa. The following story, in the present tense, captures the anxiety that farmers feel on the day they bring their cattle to auction.

The Day of Reckoning
My husband and I are at the sale barn. We have brought in our fat cattle to sell, our main income for the year. We have a farm payment to make, a note due at the bank, and other payments depending on the sale of these cattle.

We sit on the bleachers that surround the sale ring on three sides. The sawdust covered ring waits for the first animal to be brought in. The buyers are sitting together in one group. I'd seen them together before the sale in the sale barn cafeteria having coffee together. They had probably already discussed with each other how many head each one needed, so they wouldn't need to bid against each other too much. Scattered here and there among the crowd of around seventy-five people, I see other cattle producers. It is evident from the caps advertising seed corn, fertilizer, and feed that most of the crowd are farmers. I also see retired farmers who came just to pass the time. The air is becoming thick with smoke and, as they start bringing in the livestock, dust mingles with smoke.

The gate opens, and first they bring in small calves that are one week to a month old, one at a time. As each one is sold, another gate opens, and the ring man chases the calf out and bangs the gate shut. Next, they bring in the cows, with or without their calves at their sides. Then they start to bring in the fat cattle, in groups of one to around twenty, depending on how many that individual farmer had brought in. The fat cattle are separated by their size, and heifers are separated from steers. There is a scale in the sale ring, and they are sold by their weight.

Our nerves are on edge as we wait for ours to be brought in. Finally, the first group comes in. The ringman moves them around in the ring. The auctioneer starts them with a bid and gets no response. He lowers the bid, and finally the bidding starts. But wait! He said, "Sold," and that isn't enough! Three more groups come in, and the same thing. They're sold, but it isn't enough to pay all those bills already due, and those coming up in the future. We knew the price was down, it had been for three months. But the cost of the feed we bought to feed them was up. The cost of hamburger in the grocery store wasn't down. The fuel for the tractor that put in the crop of corn and made the hay to feed them had gone to near record highs. Why must we always take what they want to give us for what we have to sell? No other business can run that way. If we could figure our costs and labor on top of the value of the cattle we had sold, we and all the area farmers would be able to help keep the local businesses going. Now, as it is, we get by with as little as we can, and rural towns are dying.

Exercises
1. *Write a account of a dramatic event, such as "All that Bull," in which you are the principal actor. Write it in both the past and present tenses.*
2. *Write an account of an event to which you were a witness. Write it in both past and present tenses.*

OBSERVING THE ENVIRONMENT

Describing the world as fully as possible entails describing your environment, natural and artificial, and recording your relation to it. How you feel about that environment does not need to be stated explicitly. The reader will discover it from the tone of the work. Here is a nature observation from *Dirt & Duty*.

Lay By Time
What a luxury is late August, that lay-by season, when all the plowing, planting, spraying, chopping, cultivating are done. The crop is "laid by" because there's nothing else you can do but watch it grow. The tractors sit quietly in the shed, and I sleep late of a morning, with only the sound of birds and insects and the soft chook, chook, chook of the overhead fan. Then comes the occasional thump or bang of a tennis ball sized walnut bruising the soft earth or rattling off the tin roof shed. The first sounds of fall are pretty obvious.

Frogs retire from their chorus by sunup, their places taken by the insistent insects that provide a high, steady background whir that you only realize is there when they stop for a moment. These soft sounds are accompanied by loud solos of larger bugs that rattle the eardrum from one window to the next. Starting with first light (that dim pre-

> dawn gauze) the crows begin to caw roughly to one another in the distance. ("Get up! Quit your preening and let's eat some corn.") Blue jays squawk from the walnut top and the territorial mocking bird harangues everyone within earshot with his pronouncements. ("This is my place. I claimed it a dozen moons ago, and I have documents to prove it!")
> Time to lie back; bathed in the last night's cool dew-soaked breath; glazed by first light on new day; serenaded by all humming, chirping, squawking, trilling life as it stretches its wings.

Dirt & Duty, by the fact that it compiles a series of snapshot-like stories with meditations on rural life and nature, builds a clear and accurate picture of life on a west Tennessee farm, and in the process gives us a feel for the region's culture.

Joshua Hoyt wrote a very different kind of environment description. The excerpt that follows is not from a memoir but an essay on his work as a community organizer in Chicago, which he wrote in a writing workshop there. It forms the introduction to Joshua's essay and gives an overview of Chicago's Uptown, and how its divisions affect his work.

> Uptown, Chicago is one of those neighborhoods that look like a great urban game of multi-colored pick-up sticks thrown down on the floor. You name the fault line in America—Uptown's got it. You name the racial or immigrant group—they live in Uptown. You name the social problem or the vital activity that makes city's great—they're there in Uptown.
> The former governor's mansion is blocks from eight homeless shelters. A booming Vietnamese shopping area contains a corner where a needle exchange program for addicts, to prevent AIDS, operates on the margins of the law. Two community banks, a world renowned jazz club, three homeless shelters, a "cage hotel" flophouse, an alternative high school, a thriving community college, and a great res-

taurant share a four-block area.
   I am a community organizer. My profession is to build relationships between disconnected people. It is our relationships with others—honest, mutual, purposeful relationships—that make us human. These relationships give us power. They give us community. Ultimately, they give us meaning.
   A good organizer understands that the core of our work is the rebuilding of relationships. This gives people the power to act collectively for justice, and creates community even in a place like Uptown.
   One of the fault lines in Uptown is class—there were two sides, "us" and "them," "right" and "wrong." On one side was the business community, the real estate interests, the homeowners, the gentrifiers. On the other were the poor, the social service agencies, the immigrants, the homeless, the minorities. I met with Suellen Long, the head of the Uptown Chamber of Commerce. She was fresh from a losing attempt to close the closest homeless shelter. "How can you meet with her?" I was asked. "She's on the other side." The two "sides," sharing the same community, did not talk.

As this piece shows, an effective description of an urban environment need not rely on details of sights, sounds, and colors as we find in Stephen Crane's *Maggie*. It can be more abstract.

Exercises
1. *If you live in a rural area or have visited the countryside, reflect on a time you were especially aware of the natural surroundings and felt at one with them. It may have been an hour lying underneath a tree, a day spent canoeing or hiking in the woods. It may have been a month in the country when time slowed down and you became intimately aware of the life around you. Write about it.*
2. *If you live in an urban area or have spent time in a city, describe a street fair or neighborhood celebration, or a time you roamed city streets absorbing sights and sounds.*

3 *Pick a town or a part of a city and describe it in terms of its component parts. How do these parts relate to the people who live there?*

Process Description

Since rapid technological change is one of the most significant characteristics of our time, description of processes, past and present, are important components of memoirs. The following piece, by Gloria Blankenship, who was raised on a farm in Arkansas, describes a process that could stand on its own in a memoir. It is, however, excerpted from a longer piece about her days growing up on a Delta farm, which she wrote in the workshop in Helena, Arkansas.

> Hog killing day was a long hard day. Daddy would get a group of neighborhood men to come over to help him kill a hog. Early in the morning he would fill the old black wash pot with water and build a fire around it to get the water very hot. A metal barrel was prepared to put the hog in after it had been stabbed with a long knife to bleed and then die; bleeding was important to prevent a build up of blood in the meat. The hog was slid into the barrel, where caustic lye was put. Hot water was poured in, and the hog was turned and pulled out. Its hair was then scrapped off. Children used to stay inside during this process. We would sneak a peak through the window when Mom wasn't looking. The hog was hung up by its hind legs on a scaffold built for that purpose. The abdomen was slit open, and all the internal parts came rolling out into the #3 tub, the same tub that was used for bathing our bodies. Each part of the hog was separated. The liver was cooked for dinner that night. The intestines were washed with water pumped from the pump in the front yard and carried to the back to wash out all that stinking stuff. These would be eaten another day. We hated the process of washing the intestines—chitterlings they have now become. It is amazing how cleaning them up changed their name.
> The head was cut off, and the brain was removed. Mom

made hog head souse of it later. It was boiled, ground in the sausage grinder, seasoned and molded while it congealed in the cold. The brain was served the next morning with scrambled eggs (gathered from the hen house), hot biscuits, hot molasses and don't forget Old Bessie's butter. Backbones, neck bones, pork chops, ham, shoulders, feet, sides trimmed for salt pork-bacon. Wow! The hog was cut up! It was time to share the meat with the neighbors who had come to help kill the hog.

All of the bits and pieces of trimmed fat were either ground for sausage or put into the wash pot and cooked for crunchy cracklings. Cracklings were used to cook cornbread, a night time snack, or used to cook vegetables. Nothing from the hog was wasted. The fat from cooking the cracklings cooled to lard, used to make breads, to fry or season foods.

Descriptions of processes—how something is done—offer good material for a memoirist, especially as technologies continue to displace older hand techniques. Within the next thirty to forty years there will be few people in this country who will have had the experience Gloria describes.

As for history, even one short paragraph can convey a feeling for a different era. Murray Hudson's father, Jack Hudson, wrote his own set of memoirs for the Free River Press folk literature series, *Fishin', Farmin', Feedin', & Fightin'*. While most of his writings are anecdotal, this brief piece gives a feeling for the Great Depression in rural west Tennessee.

It would be impossible to make the young people understand just how hard times were in the early 1930's, but I think everyone enjoyed life even if it was a rough one. Back then if you worked you ate. If anyone needed help, the whole community pitched in, black or white. But if you were lazy and wouldn't work, it was a different story.

Mr. Hudson illustrated this sense of community in the following story, in which black and white families join in a fish fry. The piece is interesting on a number of levels, for it counters our usual conception of black and white relations, especially in the pre-Civil Rights era; it depicts community that no longer exists for blacks or whites; and it describes a community feast in which some of the members fish for their food while others prepare it.

The first person mentioned, Aunt Molly, was an elderly black woman. Mr. Hudson's idiosyncratic spelling and style have been left intact.

> In the summer time on the 4th of July, every one would go down to the Forked Deer River for a fish fry. Aunt Molly looked forward to the fish fry. Some one would always go after Aunt Molly and Lizzy. There would be wagons, cars, and horses every where. The women would fry country ham and make jugs of ice tea. They would bring iron kettles to cook the fish and the french fries in. There would be a pot to boil the sweet corn in. Each wagon would bring too or three planks in the bottom of the wagon bed. The men would cut poles and set them in the ground to make tables for the food, and a place to eat. The men would bring a roll of hog wire. Their was a large sand bar in the river. They would take the wire to the side of the sand bar where their was not any current. There was always some one watching to see that the small ones did not get out of the fenced in era. Kids could play in the sand and water, but if they got in the current, they would be swept down the river.
>
> Ruffus, Effus, and Grant were Aunt Molly's cousins. They always brought Aunt Molly and Lizzy. Ruffus, Effus, and Grant would not get in the river and help catch fish. They would bring the wash tubs to the river bank, the men in the river would empty the sacks of fish into the tubs. You would need two men with sacks in the water. Each time they would catch a fish, they would put it into the feed sack. Ruffus, Effus, and Grant were not going to get into the water they were ascared of the snakes.
>
> The men would use tramble nets to catch the fish. They would circle the drifts in the river with the tramble nets,

then they would get inside of the circle with punch poles and run the fish into the nets. The fish were mostly carp and buffalo, they would weigh five to ten pounds most of the time. They would catch a few yellow cats [catfish]. Some of them would weight twenty lbs.

The women all brought chairs. There were trees along the river banks, and they would set in the shade. The people would all get together or on the telephone and decide what each one should bring. They would need two stands of lard to cook the fish and french fries in. Ruffus, Effus, and Grant would clean a wash tub of fish, they would get the fires going under the wash kettles. They would have dish pans with cornmeal, salt and pepper. They would drop the pieces of fish into the corn meal and roll them around to get them covered with meal. They would drop the pieces of fish into the boiling grease. In about ten minutes the pieces of fish would rise to the top, golden brown and ready to take out of the grease and eat.

When the first tub of fish were ready to eat the women and kids would eat. They had all kinds of pickles and preserves. There is no fish as good tasting as those fresh out of the water and into the frying pan. It was hard to get the men out of the water, they enjoyed catching the fish as much as they did eating them. After the third tub full was caught they would quit, and bring the tramble net out on the bank. Effus, Ruffus and Grant had already eaten, and they would keep cooking fish as long as any one would eat them. Granddaddy would say Effus, how do the fish taste. Effus would say if they tasted any better I couldn't stand it.

This was a day of hard work, good eating and a lots of fun. Every body black and white enjoyed the day. Every one pitched in and cleaned up the camp ground. They buried all of the scraps and fish bones. They cleaned up the cooking kettles and buried the grease. By the middle of the evening every one was ready to start for home. It had been a very enjoyable day for every one.

What amazes me now is that every one has every thing

but love and happiness. In those days the people did not have much money, but they did not have a drug culture or very little crime. There was no welfare, but no one went hungry. Every one worked hard and lived off the land. If any one got sick and needed help, the whole neighborhood would get together and help the family out. Those were the kind of people that settled the county, fought the wars and made the country great. During the great depression times were hard, no one had any money, but every one was in the same boat and you did the best you could and most people were happy. It's not that way with the next generation. They have everything and are bored with life.

Unlike the short anecdotes which his son Murray used to compose *Dirt & Duty*, Mr. Hudson wrote chunks of stories tied together by common themes, such as fishing, hunting, farming, and so on. These chunks were later broken into their component stories and arranged chronologically. If you have not written your memoir in relatively short pieces, begin the editing process by breaking your larger sections into their component parts.

> *Exercise*
> Write an account of a process. Perhaps the process is a skill you have, such as furniture making or painting. Perhaps it is a process you have observed over a period of time, such as the construction of a skyscraper or the erosion of a hillside.

Arranging Stories Chronologically

Once you have most of your stories written, and have broken them into their component parts, arrange them chronologically. The reason for ordering them in time is to gain an understanding of yourself and thereby understand what your book is about. Many years ago someone said to me that the reason we write autobiography is to find meaning in our lives. I believe this is true. We may find, or think we find, meaning in a surface account of activity: a life spent accumulating money or real estate, spent in hazardous adventure, or in the accumulation of power. Bookstore shelves do not lack for want of books of this kind written by politicians or celebrities. But we may find meaning to our lives in the development of our character or understanding. Since development depends upon linear time, your stories, reflections, and anecdotes should be arranged chronologically.

DETERMINING A THEME

The most challenging memoir I worked on began as a 350-page manuscript called *A Rogues Island Memoir*, by Rod Haynes. Rod's first draft covered the first twenty-six years of his life, but eventually it became clear that the story's proper end came the summer after high school, and he cut the book's last two sections. It took five months of work on the early drafts before this became evident.

The immediate problem with the manuscript was the fact that it was written in the manner of Jack Hudson's reminiscences, in chapters unified by subject. Hence the writing jumped back and forth in time. The reader would have spent many hours reading and rereading the chapters before he understood what held things together. But Rod had provided a one-page synopsis of themes, which stated explicitly and concisely some of what he intended to convey.

> While it wasn't perfect, my early life in Lime Rock had a sweet, dream-like quality to it until 1968, the year my fourteen-year-old sister Jen died. From that time forward most everything went to hell.
> Jen was the "jewel" in our family's "crown." Finding it impossible to cope with her death, my family quickly lost our way individually and collectively, spiraling down into a long, painful period of doubt and self-destruction. We became stuck in the ugly, dark tar pit of a nation at war with itself and with enemies abroad. While the external madness of that period swirled all around us, inside the protective cocoon of the 1960s southern New England suburbia my

family sought our own separate corners to comfort ourselves in our grief and anger.

My family did not know how to communicate our sense of loss and frustration over Jen's death with each other, so eventually we fell apart. And so did the nation. In late 1968 without knowing I was doing it I bade farewell to my childhood, my older sister, and the northern Rhode Island village I knew and loved as a child all at about the same time. Looking back, I guess life has a way of balancing things out, where the good times are evened out by the realities of life. Some say you can't remain a kid forever. But there's more to this story than that.

This became the starting point for a fuller elaboration of themes and story line. The synopsis tells two things: first, that the author's life had "a dream-like quality" until his sister's death; second, that after her death his family lost "their way individually and collectively" and "eventually fell apart." Her death, in other words, was the pivotal event in the family's life.

This gives us a strong opening for the drama. It gives us an event which upsets the equilibrium of the characters' world. Each of Shakespeare's plays opens with a jarring scene, often violent. These scenes bring disorder, and it is the protagonist's job—in history, tragedy, and comedy—to restore equilibrium. With more information from Rod I began to envision a shape for his book. It began by portraying Home, then the loss of Home, and concluded with the search for a new Home. The rest of the business of writing—deciding which anecdotes and stories related to this theme and revising them, and cutting those which did not—depended on this foundation. While the book does not end with equilibrium restored, it points towards it.

Deciding Which Stories to Include

Whether you write your memoir in discrete anecdotes or try tackling larger units, you are eventually faced with the task of discovering what your book is about. Simply because something happened to you does not mean it belongs in your memoirs. Each story or anecdote has to contribute to the major story line, which is intertwined with the theme. All parts of the work—anecdote, process description, meditation, character description— must be subordinated to it. Each part of the book must contribute to the life of the whole. If your first draft lacks a visible connecting thread, you must discover one. The thread is the journey you have taken.

Inevitably, your memoir will have stories that illustrate the character of various persons. If they played a pivotal role in your development, include them. But a story about your seventh-grade shop teacher, though he may have been eccentric or funny, is not a candidate for inclusion unless he influenced your life. Nor is the story of a wonderful afternoon spent at a waterfall in remote woods, unless it offers a contrast with other parts of the narrative. Let us say that you are in the process of writing about a difficult period in your life. If within that period you had a day of respite, a day of calm and peace within the surrounding storm, then it belongs in the memoir by the fact that it offers the reader a release of tension.

As you assemble your anecdotes, thoughts, and meditations, constantly think back to the big picture, the theme of your work. It is the theme which will determine what stays and goes. Making the decision to cut various stories is often the most difficult part of the writing process because emotional attachment to certain episodes may make it difficult to see that they are irrelevant. This is where sympathetic readers can be helpful. However, a reader who means well but does not know how to offer constructive criticism without negative baggage can bring the work to a halt. You can limit the potential for destructive comments by making clear to the reader that you only want to know if stories are relevant or not. Once irrelevancies are removed, your work will be strengthened by the fact that the story line—the emotional through line—is clarified.

CHAPTER SEVEN
GROUP ACTIVITIES

The activities described in this chapter are among my favorites, mostly because I have enormous fun working with non-competitive groups to create a play, a scenario, or a novel. Such projects not only can be fun, the right group can offer the student insights into dialogue and structure that he might not acquire on his own.

Aside from the application of the group exercises to fiction and playwriting, the major focus of the present chapter is on understanding stock types and situations that we find throughout literature. The importance of understanding recurrent characters, plots and situations cannot be over-emphasized. For if the student is freed from the burden of having to invent his own, then he finds much of his creativity and energy going into other facets of the work, not into reinventing the wheel. This is not to say that great or good writing is done by formula. On the contrary, too much attention to conventions can lead to over-calculation and paralysis. But we do need to remember that the greatest English-speaking writer seldom, if ever, invented his own plots and characters. I believe there are at most two or three of Shakespeare's plays whose sources have eluded scholarly identification.

The examples in this chapter are taken largely from theater, in part because the stock types are readily apparent there, and because playwrights have frequently rewritten or adapted one another's works. A study of literary conventions does well to begin with theater, and then extend to novels and other literary forms.

WRITING WORKSHOPS

Before dealing with literary forms, however, we need to think first about group dynamics. A good writing workshop or collaborative group is nurturing, and everyone who is willing to "play the game" benefits. The nurturing workshop is one in which all members actually care about everyone else's writing. They encourage one another when spirits flag, and they know how to draw good material from one another.

The destructive workshop is one in which a significant portion of the members are there for themselves alone. One such type attends workshops to display the enormity of their talent. They can go on and on about themselves and their work, wasting everybody's time, including their own. Another negative type is the hyper-intelligent critic who can tell you everything wrong with your work. His own productions are close to flawless, perhaps in need of a bit of retouching here and there but nothing more. A group with several of this type of "expert" makes a workshop less than productive. Negative criticism can disable you.

A writing workshop needs at least one member whose work others respect, who encourages them, and sets the tone. It may be an instructor or a facilitator; in either event she needs to make clear that negative comments are not allowed. For example, it does not do a writer any good simply to say, "Your dialogue is unbelievable." That does nothing to help the writer understand the elements of good dialogue and to get her started writing it. It merely stops the writing process.

A supportive group will discover the pattern underlying the unsuccessful dialogue. Perhaps the rhythms do not vary or the characters explain too much. Whatever the cause, it needs to be treated as a group problem, one which every member will encounter. When approached in this spirit, a workshop member can suggest an adjustment. The proposed solution should be tested with everyone's participation. A facilitator or instructor who does not understand the destructive potential of negative comments is inadvertently as damaging as a highly competitive writer. If you find yourself in a group of writers who thrive on criticism, or with a group whose instructor or facilitator does not oppose negative criticism, you will be better off finding another group or working on your own.

PARODYING POPULAR GENRES

Writing a group parody of a popular genre is an easy way to begin thinking about literary conventions and consciously using them, while at the same time making the learning process a game. Of the several methods I have used to study genres and conventions, the following is the loosest and most informal. I first saw a product of the method in Santa Fe, New Mexico where every year on Labor Day weekend, the Santa Fe Community Theater produces a melodrama written in group collaboration.

I was enormously entertained by the first one I saw, and a few years later I happily became one of the regular, albeit minor, writers on the yearly project. About eight of us would gather once a week, first to create the outline or scenario for the script, and then to write the dialogue. It was a fairly anarchic exercise, with everyone shouting out lines. If you weren't on the inside track with the group, your lines were usually ignored by the woman who recorded dialogue. Each year the plays would pack the 150-seat theater with people standing shoulder to shoulder in the aisles for six performances. Like a good melodrama audience they roared encouragement and sympathy to the innocent and dimwitted hero and heroine, and booed the conniving villain and his tainted girlfriend as they went about their nefarious business. Since melodrama was a popular tradition in Santa Fe, people knew the stock characters, plots, and situations. Concocting a suitable story was never a great problem. Dialogue writing was aided by the fact that everyone was familiar with B westerns and could borrow appropriate lines. It was community theater in the true sense.

When you use this process, begin by picking a popular genre familiar to the group. Whatever it is—mystery story, detective yarn, romantic comedy—exaggeration is the key to successful parody. Recall how successful film spoofs rely upon exaggeration. Think of the *Pink Panther* series, in which Peter Sellers plays an inept Interpol investigator, a parody of Agatha Christie's Hercule Poirot. Recall the *Naked Gun* series, which parodied the detective genre itself. Think of Mel Brooks's two most notable films, *Blazing Saddles* and *Young Frankenstein,* which were parodies of the western and monster film respectively.

Whatever genre your group chooses, base your protagonist on a recognizable hero, perhaps a film celebrity who specializes in a genre. Ask what your protagonist is trying to do. Break a vicious drug ring? Save Earth from alien invaders? Marry a vivacious blonde? When you have decided his or her objective, a one-sentence story line will suggest itself, and because a story has opposition, you will, almost simultaneously, develop an antagonist—the head of the drug ring, the alien leader, the rival in love. Drawing on your knowledge of the kinds of episodes the genre demands, begin to create situations. As you pick ones you like, a plot suggests itself. Write brief one or two paragraph descriptions of the activity in each scene. Above each paragraph write where the action occurs, and the time of day, if important. For example:

The State Capitol. Senator Duffy's office. Noon.
Senator Duffy's aide is on the phone, explaining the senator's position on abortion to a reporter. Duffy enters. The aid gets off the phone fast and tells his boss they have a problem. *The Daily Times* wants an interview. They discuss how to put a spin on his latest public statement, which aroused protest. Duffy leaves to meet with an ally, Senator Jones.

When you have finished writing the story out in this fashion, begin improvising dialogue while someone writes it down. Periodically stop and read what has been recorded. Revise it. Proceed to more dialogue.

You may not finish your play. You may decide after four scenes to bring the exercise to a close. What is most important here is process, not result. Once result becomes paramount the exercise ceases to be a game. In addition to exploring a genre, the purpose of the exercise is to allow each member to participate. One way to prevent one or two people from dominating the proceedings is to appoint a facilitator who will call upon the most vociferous to take time out, and to signal when a suggestion by a quieter member should be incorporated.

Exercise
With three or more people, pick a genre for a one-act play. Create a hero based upon a typical protagonist in the genre. Develop a one-paragraph story line and discover the antagonist. Isolate typical situations in the genre. Pick the ones that most appeal to you and fit within the story. Construct your plot. Then improvise your dialogue. Record it, and at the next meeting read it back. Rewrite it.

CREATING SCENARIOS

One of the best places to begin examining stock types, standard plots, and conventions is the commedia dell'arte, the improvised Italian comedy of the seventeenth century. Here we have a handful of characters repeated in play after play in standardized plots mixing romance with raucous buffoonery. Each commedia actor played one character for life, and the plays themselves were improvised from scenarios. A scenario describes the outline of a play, giving the gist of the action for each scene. Each unit of the scenario looks like the paragraph about Senator Duffy in the previous section. A story line for a play or novel that is described in a series of such capsule scenes is a scenario

The commedia's characters reach back to ancient Greece and ever since have been continuously reincarnated, not only in theater, but in novels, film, and television. *Seinfeld*'s Cosmo Kramer, for example, is a modern-day Arlequino. The parodies of fire-eating German generals whom the British love to portray are contemporary versions of Capitano Spivento, the braggart soldier. And every literary portrayal of the pompous academic is a version of the commedia's Dr. Gratiano. The correspondences are legion. But the commedia did not invent these characters, and we can trace may of them back to Aristophanes and Menander.

Canadian critic Northrop Frye's books *The Educated Imagination* and *The Anatomy of Criticism* provide a theory of myths and types that encompasses all western literary forms (e.g. novels and plays) and genres within a form (e.g. the romance novel and the detective novel). Frye identifies character types, plots, and conventions recurring across centuries and between forms. Other critics have made similar identifications. In terms of recurrent plots, think of all the stories from the Bible that have been adapted into verse and fiction. Consider that Goethe's *Faust* was inspired by Marlowe's *Dr. Faustus,* and that Marlowe's play was adapted from a German story. Consider that Shakespeare's *Coriolanus* was an adaptation of Plutarch's biography, and that Brecht likewise used it for his own version of the story. The multiplication of examples continues indefinitely, and a study of them helps dispel the notion that a creative artist creates *ex nihil,* from nothing. One begins to see that a novel or story based on a preestablished plot, one that has been used and readapted over centuries, has an excellent base. And one also begins to see that characters that are conscious adaptations (not apings) of a type, likewise have a solid base.

Contemporary commedia experiments offer the opportunity to go to the heart of comedy and from there branch out to a study of conventions and types in other forms. A group essay into adaptation provides creative and critical training simultaneously. Creating a scenario, which can be used either as the skeleton of a play or novel, will have you adapting old plots and stock types to contemporary times.

In the mid-1980s I worked with a group of actors and writers to create a contemporary American commedia, adapting the stock types to today, and creating scenarios with contemporary place and situations. Our first step in creating our theater was to write our scenarios. Instead of writing them from scratch, we reversed the process of the previous exercise. Instead of beginning with characters we began with a story. Each of us read two or three Grimm's folk tales and reported back to the group with a summary of each. Several of us had chosen "The Goose Girl," which we liked because it seemed to lend itself easily to adaptation. It became the basis for our first scenario.

"The Goose Girl" tells of a princess who leaves home with her lady-in-waiting to travel to the land of the prince who is her betrothed. On the journey the lady-in-waiting forces the princess to trade clothes so that she, the lady-in-waiting, can present herself to the prince as his bride. On arrival the lady-in-waiting is greeted as the bride-to-be while the princess is given the chore of tending geese. The lady-in-waiting asks the prince to kill the princess's horse and spike its head to the castle gate. The horse's head, however, is able to speak and reveals the truth. The lady-in-waiting is killed, and the prince and princess are married, and the princess's horse is restored to life.

In modernizing "The Goose Girl" we would need a princess, and what better than a spoiled, rich, young lady? She would marry a real prince, who ruled a country we called Caledonia. Our modern-day lady-in-waiting would of course be a maid, and a look alike of her boss. Fed up with constant orders, she would try to dispose of her employer and marry the prince in her stead. But that did not seem enough. We complicated the story with the addition of another look alike, and gave the prince an evil twin who, with the backing of the CIA, deposed his brother. Since we were going to use masks, we would not have a problem convincing an audience of the likelihood of mistaken identities.

Two meetings after presenting the synopses of our folk tales, we had established enough elements of our scenario to begin writing. The finished piece is a farce, and as an exercise it was fun. Gibson's book, *Shakespeare's Game*, had pointed out that each of Shakespeare's plays started off with an event, often violent, which disturbed the equilibrium of the characters' world. With this in mind, we began our story with a coup in which the evil twin deposed his brother, the prince.

CHARACTERS
Judy, a spoiled rich, young lady
Maria, her maid, a look alike of Judy
the Prince of Caledonia
the Prince's evil twin brother
the American ambassador, also a CIA operative
guards, assassins

SCENE ONE. *Caledonia. The palace.*
he American ambassador sneaks on stage, looks around. The coast is clear. He looks behind him and waves. Armed assassins appear and follow him furtively across stage and off. They reappear dragging the prince, who is shouting to be

released. They leave, and the prince's evil twin appears and laughs: "Now I am prince of Caledonia!"

SCENE TWO. *America. Judy's luxury apartment.*
Judy and Maria enter. Maria is reading a letter out loud. The letter is from Judy's fiancé, the prince of Caledonia. It is evident from the letter that the marriage has been arranged and that the two have never met.

Maria takes a photograph of the prince from the letter. Judy says she is delighted to have finally met someone worthy of her and dictates a letter to the prince. When she finishes, she gives Maria a photograph of herself to include in the letter. She then gives Maria work to do and leaves for her health club.

SCENE THREE. *Caledonia. The torture room beneath the palace.*
The prince's evil twin, now wearing the prince's military uniform, is torturing the prince, who is bound to a rack.
The evil twin tells the prince that he helped the revolution because he has hated his brother since childhood. Their mother and father, he says, always gave the prince the best of everything and gave him leftovers. Now he taunts his brother with the fact that he is going to marry his fiance.

And so it proceeds. Each adaptation is a form of transformation. Some preserve few aspects of the original, others correspond part by part. As you construct your adaptation, be careful not to lose sight of the original. The reason for adaptation is to preserve a story line and the essence of characters that have proved successful.

Exercise
Between everyone in your group, read six to a dozen folk tales and pick one to adapt. Decide which characters and situations you do not want to use and find equivalents for the rest. Begin the action with a

disruptive situation. Write your story line, then break it into scenes. For each scene, write where it happens, who is present, and the gist of the action.

STATUS GAMES

British playwright and actor Keith Johnstone made some important discoveries about character and scene work in the process of conducting mask classes for members of the National Theater of Britain. But what he discovered is useful not only for the incipient playwright but for the apprentice novelist and short story writer as well. One particular aspect of Johnstone's work, the study of status, is particularly useful. Johnstone divides characters into high, middle, and low status and analyzes their relationships in terms of power. A low status individual defers to middle and high status characters, while high status defers to neither, and middle defers to high and expects subservience from low. Since status and power relationships often determine the outcome of personal interaction, giving time to think about status and power and their relation to character is time well spent.

Those of us in the commedia theater project took a workshop with a master mask instructor, who had us playing one of Johnstone's status games. The Three Stooges, the instructor pointed out, were an example of the three levels of rank. Moe is high status, Larry is middle, and Curly is low. If something goes wrong, Moe will poke Larry in the eyes and Larry will bonk Curly. If Larry thinks about bonking Moe, all Moe has to do is screw-up his face and give Larry a nasty look for Larry to back down.

In the status game we played, the middle status character was the foreman at a company where the low status character worked the assembly line. The high status character owned the factory. The high and low status characters had to maintain a consistent attitude throughout the scene. The high status character was always domineering and the low status character was always obsequious. The middle status character, however, had to be obsequious with high status but domineering with low. When all three were on stage he had had to switch his attitude and behavior constantly. He would be ordered about by the owner and grovel on the floor, then would turn and roar at the low status worker who in turn would cringe. As the tempo of the scene increased, so did the frenzy of the middle status character as he assumed one attitude, then the other. Finally he collapsed on the floor.

While this example is primitive, in its essence it holds the gist for an indefinite number of other scenes, of varying sophistication. The possibilities for a status-oriented scene are complicated when you add more than one character of each status to it. A courtroom novel or drama offers the potential for conflict among the lawyers, each vying for highest status. While status is not the defining element of character, it is an important one, and one on which other characteristics can be layered.

Exercise
Have the group pick three characters—high, middle and low status. Define who they are and what they do and how they are connected. Perhaps they live in the same town or work together. Perhaps they are in the same army platoon in wartime. Write a scene or story with all three.

ONE STEP FURTHER

One of Shakespeare's earliest works, *Henry VI, Part One*, is a collaboration which shows the hand of at least three writers. One author, who has strong command of blank verse, opens it.

> Hung be the heavens with black, yield day to night!
> Comets, importing change of times and states,
> Brandish your crystal tresses in the sky;

The scene which follows, is written in lines that falter.

> Mars his true moving, even as in the heavens
> So in the earth, to this day is not known:
> Late did he shine upon the English side;
> Now we are victors, upon us he smiles.

The iambic pulse is gone, the phrasing is awkward. Rhythmically it is a hash. These first two writers share the bulk of the play between them. The third hand writes in couplets, and appears in act four.

> The sword of Orleans hath not made me smart;
> These words of yours draw life-blood from my heart:
> On that advantage, bought with such a shame,
> To save a paltry life, and slay bright fame,
> Before young Talbot from old Talbot fly,
> The coward horse that bears me fall and die!

Elizabethan playwrights collaborated frequently. The fact that the Globe company, according to Bernard Beckerman, produced fifteen to sixteen plays a season between Easter and Christmas, including revivals, meant that collaboration was needed to meet the public's demand for new works. Judging from the evidence of *Henry VI, Part One* and other plays, collaboration between the Elizabethans meant that they outlined their play, then wrote a scenario, and divided the scenes among themselves.

The nature of Elizabethan collaboration inspired me to attempt that same method with playwriting students. This experiment also involved scenario writing but a great deal of analysis. I wanted the class to study dramatic structure and character types through the study of one genre. It was a more sophisticated and analytical version of the melodrama parody. The class read and analyzed about half a dozen of one genre's best examples, isolated their main characteristics and then collaborated. Using Restoration and eighteenth-century comedies for our model, we took five plays for the exercise: Congreve's *The Way of the World* and T*he Double-Dealer;* Sheridan's *School for Scandal* and *The Rivals,* and Goldsmith's *She Stoops to Conquer.* Each of us picked one play and read it, then wrote an in-depth scenario. We accompanied the scenario with a succinct plot summary of our play and a phrase or sentence describing each character. We also listed the important features of our play, such as wit, adultery, and double-crossing. We read all of our scenarios aloud and isolated nine common dramatic elements which we summarized as follows:

1) people slandering others to achieve their own ends;
2) young lovers pitted against parents or guardians;
3) mistaken identities;
4) people pretending to hate the object of their lust;
5) fortune hunting;
6) manipulating others for personal gain;
7) making others appear ridiculous;
8) misinterpreting signals;
9) adultery or attempted adultery.

The typical characters of these comedies were:

1) the charming wastrel (often the hero);
2) the innocent ward or love child (the heroine);
3) the pompous ass;
4) the heroine's stern and wealthy guardian;
5) the impeccable citizen;
6) the schemer (woman or man);
7) the temptress;
8) the virtuous dull, young man;
9) the wife of the guardian;
10) the antagonist.

To avoid the problems attendant on creating a new plot, we based our scenario and characters for the most part on *The Double-Dealer* and set our play in a New England theological seminary. But because we placed our characters in an academic setting, a different plot eventually emerged.

Again, the strength of this exercise lies in group investigation. The point is not simply to write a scenario, and use that as the basis of a novel or play. That is one of the goals; the other is to investigate a genre of novels or plays and learn more about its types, plots, and conventions. One could, for example, read several short novels in a genre, perhaps the novels of a single author, isolate their characteristics, and imitate his work. Or one could choose several novelists or short story writers and follow the method outlined earlier. Whichever path you choose, maintain the spirit of play.

Exercise
Pick a genre of plays, novels, or stories with which your group is not familiar. Between all of you, read a half a dozen examples of the genre. Identify its character types and stock situations. Pick one or two examples of the genre and create an archetypal plot and characters. Write your scenario, divide it among the group, and begin writing.

A GROUP NOVEL

A method for group novel writing that works with a very large group—possibly as many as 40 people—is to have four or five members decide in advance on the genre and create the characters and scenario.

I devised this method when I was asked by communications staff members at Iowa State University to run a writing workshop for the 2003 annual Agricultural Communications Conference they were hosting. They wanted the workshop to offer a creative option for conference attendees. I suggested that since the workshop went for one-and-a-half days, that we have workshop members collaborate on a novel.

Here is an excerpt from the tongue-in-cfheek introduction to the novel, *Pulp Feathers*, that they wrote and Free River Press published.

> As for how I set things up, I told the organizers—Cooper, Edwards, Meyer, and Karen Bolluyt—that we would begin by devising a scenario the writers would follow. A scenario is a scene-by-scene outline of a play or novel, giving the gist of the action and dialogue for each episode. By limiting each scene description to one or two paragraphs, we avoided cramping what the writers considered their creativity. However, by giving them a general description of each character and by handing them the story outline, we simplified our project by making this mystery novel a kind of write-by-numbers book. Connecting the dots was up to the "creative talent."

I can handle up to twenty people in a writing workshop, because with any more than that the gum snapping is distracting. The idea was to get our people on a real assembly line, and since writers are basically people with low IQs and big egos, they snapped up as much work as they could handle. We grouped them around a large square of tables, each one with a laptop. We read the scenario aloud and discussed our characters. To get everyone in the mood, we read aloud portions from a few schlock novels and discussed the elements of the best-seller style. Then everyone picked a chapter from the scenario and set to work. They wrote for perhaps an hour and a half before reading their drafts for comments. When these were intelligible or intelligent, the writers usually revised. For a day and a half we proceeded in this fashion until everyone had written at least one, and in some cases two, chapters.

Exercise
1) If you belong to a writing group that can meet for a full day, set a time limit to each part of this exercise. Take fifteen minutes to pick a genre. Take, say, another fifteen minutes to create the precipitating circumstance that gets the action going: a body is found, a boy meets a girl, a bank is robbed. Next, decide on your major characters and their relation to the precipitating circumstance. Now you devise your plot and from that create a scenario.
    Limit yourselves to a 100-page novella. Let each member of the group choose the chapter he wants to write. Finish your first drafts the first day and read them to the group. Take comments and before the next group meeting, incorporate some. Read your rewrites at the next meeting. Take more comments and complete the rewrites.
Continue this process until you have completed at least two drafts of the novella. If done in a cooperative spirit, in which no one is the last word, the process is simply good play.

SUGGESTED READINGS

Anderson, Sherwood. *Winesburg, Ohio*. New York: Viking Press, 1974.
Crane, Stephen. *Maggie and Other Stories*. New York: Washington Square Press, 1960.
Dunne, Peter Finley. *Mr. Dooley Says*. Project Guttenburg, 2005.
Elbow, Peter. *Writing Without Teachers*. New York: Oxford University Press, 1974, 1998.
Gibson, William. *Shakespeare's Game*. New York: Atheneum, 1978.
Gilbert, El. *Lion's Share*. Nashville: Free River Press, 1990.
Harris, Joel Chandler. *Old Plantation Stories*. Boston: Houghton-Mifflin, 1920.
Haynes, Rod. *Rogue's Island Memoir*. Lansing, Iowa: Free River Press, 2000.
Hudson, Murray. *Dirt & Duty*. Lansing, Iowa: Free River Press, 1995.
Kerouac, Jack. *The Subterraneans*, New York: Grove Press, 1958.
_____. "The Railroad Earth." In *Lonesome Traveler*. New York: McGraw-Hill, 1960.
Pound, Ezra. *The ABC of Reading*. New York: New Directions, 1963.
_____. "Cathay." In *Ezra Pound: Translations*. New York: New Directions, 1963.
Runyon, Damon. *Dream Street*. London: Folio Society, 1989.
Sandburg, Carl. *Chicago Poems*. New York: Henry Holt and Company, 1916.
Shepherd, Jean. *In God We Trust All Others Pay Cash*. Garden City: Doubleday & Company, 19072.
Wolf, Robert. *An American Mosaic*. New York: Oxford University Press, 1999.
_____. *Heartland Portrait*, 2nd ed. Decorah, Iowa: Free River

www.ingramcontent.com/pod-product-compliance
Lightning Source LLC
Chambersburg PA
CBHW050556300426
44112CB00013B/1946